Try It, You'll Like It!
Microwaved

Cover picture:

Iclandic Vinertarta
Pineapple Sunburst Cheesecake
Fresh Fruit Ring

Photography by:
Ross Durant, Vancouver, B.C.

Food Styling by
Eileen Dwillies, Vancouver, B.C.

Prop Coordination by
Valerie Bedwell, Vancouver, B.C.

We wish to thank TUPPERWARE CANADA and TUPPERWARE
U.S.A. for their generous donation of Ultra 21 Ovenware.
We also wish to thank the following Vancouver retail outlets for
their donation of dishes, glassware and accessories — Designer
Furniture Galleries, Hollingdale's, Lighting Land, Mikasa, Pres-
ents of Mind, and Terra Cotta Gallery.

Susan VanderVelde
Joyce Webster

First Printing — September 1987

Includes index.

ISBN 0-9693094-0-6

Printed by D. W. Friesen & Sons Ltd.
Altona, Manitoba CANADA

Table Of Contents

Cooking for One and Two   1

Bread, Muffins and Coffeecakes 19

Cakes 33

Bars, Slices and Squares 55

Pies, Tarts and Cheesecakes 68

Puddings and Desserts 86

Cookies 105

Frozen Desserts 110

Frostings and Icings 115

Sauces, Jams and Syrups 119

Candies 128

Slightly Gourmet 134

Notes From Authors

While researching recipes for TRY IT, YOU'LL LIKE IT, MICROWAVED, we found it was a delightful experience reading cookbooks dating back to the early 1900's. That was a time when measurements consisted of a ''gill'' of water, a ''teacupful of flour'' or a ''handful'' of raisins. The cooking instructions simply read ''Cook'' or ''Cook over a hot fire''. Although those were quaint instructions, we would be at a loss to understand them today.

Some of those forgotton ''Golden Oldies'' will bring back fond memories of delicious desserts, that your mother or perhaps grandmother used to make. Our recipes and methods have been updated for microwave cooking with easy to follow instructions.

These recipes have been tested on 700 watt output ovens. If your oven output differs, (the wattage will be on the back of your microwave) you may have to adjust your time accordingly. Undercook rather than overcook. We have stated in most recipes whether or not to cover.

TRY IT, YOU'LL LIKE IT! MICROWAVED!

Best Wishes,

Susan VanderVelde and Joyce Webster

Cooking for One or Two

No need to compromise on the variety of desserts you serve just because you are cooking for one or two. Cooking small quantities can be fun and easy with the speed of the microwave. The recipes in this section have been developed for smaller quantities and can be prepared with a minimum of time and effort.

How often have you wanted a piece of chocolate layer cake or a slice of pie but didn't want to have leftovers for the rest of the week? With these recipes, you can be creative and treat yourself to a variety of desserts. Take 2 minutes to microwave a cup of sauce or fruit filling and store in the refrigerator. This can be used in a variety of ways to prepare an elegant dessert. The fillings can be used for tarts, crepes, and cakes. Sauces can be served over ice cream, fruit desserts and puddings. These are just a few ideas to help you create your own specialty.

Spicy Currant Muffins

Take a couple of these to work for your coffee break. Better still, take the batter to work and microwave them fresh!

½ cup	flour	125 mL
⅓ cup	brown sugar	75 mL
1 tsp.	baking powder	5 mL
½ tsp.	salt	2 mL
¼ tsp.	allspice	1 mL
¼ tsp.	mace	1 mL
¼ tsp.	cinnamon	1 mL
½ cup	currants or raisins	125 mL
⅓ cup	milk	75 mL
1	egg	1
1 tsp.	vanilla	5 mL

1. Combine flour, brown sugar, baking powder, salt, spices and currants. Mix well.

2. In a separate bowl, combine milk, egg and vanilla and beat until frothy. Add liquid to dry ingredients and stir until smooth. Do not overmix.

3. Place 6 large muffin liners in a muffin pan and spoon batter evenly into each.

4. Microwave uncovered, on MEDIUM HIGH 3½ to 4 minutes.

Yields 6 muffins.

Microtip
This batter may be doubled; bake 6 muffins at a time.

Jam Filled Muffins

A tasty treat for Sunday brunch. The next best thing to jelly donuts.

¼ cup	butter	60 mL
¼ cup	sugar	60 mL
1	egg, beaten	1
2 tbsp.	milk	30 mL
¾ cup	flour	175 mL
1 tsp.	baking powder	5 mL
	jam	
2 tbsp.	melted butter	30 mL
3 tbsp.	sugar	45 mL
¼ tsp.	cinnamon	1 mL

1. In a mixing bowl, cream butter and sugar together, add egg and milk.

2. Combine flour and baking powder and blend into butter mixture.

3. Line a microwave muffin pan with 4 large muffin papers. Spoon HALF the batter evenly into each muffin cup. Place a teaspoon of jam over the batter. Top with remaining muffin batter and micro-wave on HIGH 2½ to 3 minutes.

4. Combine sugar and cinnamon together. As soon as muffins are cooked, brush top of each with melted butter and sprinkle with cinnamon/sugar mixture. Serve warm with butter. MMMM Good!

Yields 4 large muffins.

See photo, page 9.

Microtip
The jam will be very hot at first. Let cool a couple of minutes before eating.

Apricot Fig Loaf

Need a gift in a hurry? Try this loaf, you'll like it! Make enough batter for two or three loaves and freeze them. Nice to have on hand. Bake only one at a time.

¹/₂ cup	chopped dried apricots	125 mL
¹/₂ cup	water	125 mL
¹/₂ cup	chopped Calimara Figs	125 mL
³/₄ cup	white flour	175 mL
³/₄ cup	whole wheat flour	175 mL
¹/₄ tsp.	salt	1 mL
1¹/₂ tsp.	baking powder	7 mL
³/₄ cup	brown sugar	175 mL
1	egg	1
¹/₂ cup	milk	125 mL
1 tbsp.	melted butter	15 mL

1. Combine apricots and water. Microwave on HIGH, covered, one minute. Add chopped figs, stir and set aside.

2. Combine flours, salt, baking powder and sugar.

3. In a separate bowl, beat together egg, milk and melted butter.

4. Blend egg mixture into flour and add chopped fruit.

5. Line a 4 cup microwave loaf pan with wax paper and spoon batter evenly into the pan. Cover and microwave 3¹/₂ to 4¹/₂ minutes on HIGH. Let stand uncovered 5 minutes before turning out. Loaf slices better when cool. This is a real treat when toasted!

Yields one loaf.

Variation
If you aren't going to toast this loaf, you could pour a thin fruit glaze over the top while still warm.

See photo, page 9.

Colonial Fruit Bread

Conventionally this would take an hour to bake, in the microwave it takes less than 5 minutes!!!! Colonial Fruit Bread is excellent toasted. Due to the density of these ingredients, this should be microwaved in a small, 4 cup loaf pan.

³/₄ cup	white flour	175 mL
³/₄ cup	whole wheat flour	175 mL
¹/₄ tsp.	salt	1 mL
1¹/₂ tsp.	baking powder	7 mL
¹/₄ tsp.	cloves	1 mL
¹/₂ tsp.	cinnamon	2 mL
¹/₂ tsp.	nutmeg	2 mL
³/₄ cup	brown sugar	175 mL
1	egg	1
¹/₂ cup	milk	125 mL
1 tbsp.	melted butter	15 mL
¹/₄ cup	chopped raisins	60 mL
¹/₄ cup	chopped candied peel	60 mL
¹/₄ cup	chopped candied cherries	60 mL
1 tbsp.	water	15 mL
¹/₄ cup	chopped nuts	60 mL

1. Combine the flours, salt, baking powder, spices and sugar.

2. In a separate container, mix together, egg, milk and melted butter. Add to flour mixture.

3. In a small bowl, combine raisins, peel and cherries. Add 1 tbsp. water and microwave 1 minute on HIGH, covered, to soften fruit.

4. Combine fruit and nuts with batter. This will be fairly thick.

5. Line a 4 cup loaf pan with wax paper. Spoon batter evenly into pan, smoothing the top.

6. Microwave, covered, on HIGH 3¹/₂ to 4¹/₂ minutes. Test for doneness with a wooden skewer. Let stand 5 minutes before turning out. See photo page 9.

Yields one loaf.

Microtip
If the loaf is slightly undercooked on the bottom, place the loaf back in the pan, cover, turn pan upside down and microwave an additional 30 to 60 seconds.

Quick Raisin Bread For Two

From start to finish, if your ingredients are handy, this can be made in 5 minutes!

1¼ cups	Bisquick	310 mL
¼ cup	milk	60 mL
1	egg	1
¼ cup	sugar	60 mL
½ tsp.	cinnamon	2 mL
⅛ tsp.	cloves	pinch
⅓ cup	chopped raisins	75 mL

1. Combine all ingredients thoroughly. Place in a four cup (1 L) loaf pan. Microwave uncovered, on HIGH 3 minutes. This is best when toasted.

Yields one small loaf.

Variation
Combine 2 tbsp. crushed walnuts, 1 tbsp. brown sugar and ½ tsp. cinnamon. Sprinkle on top of bread before cooking.

Rice Pudding

1 cup	cooked rice	250 mL
1	egg	1
¼ cup	milk	60 mL
½ tsp.	vanilla	2 mL
pinch	salt	pinch
1 tbsp.	sugar	15 mL
pinch	cinnamon	pinch

1. In a mixing bowl, combine all of the above ingredients. Spoon into two serving bowls.

2. Cover and microwave both desserts on MEDIUM LOW 3–4 minutes or until set. Serve with cream or 2 tbsp. melted jam of any flavor.

Apples With Cranberry Sauce

One of the 'Minute Marvel' quickie desserts that are so popular with microwave owners. The Cranberry Sauce adds superb flavor and color.

2	apples, peeled and cored	2
¼ cup	Cranberry Orange Sauce	60 mL

1. Place each apple in an attractive stemmed glass and spoon 2 tbsp. Cranberry Sauce over each apple. Cover and microwave 2 to 3 minutes for both apples or 1 to 1½ minutes for one.

Serves 2.

Variation
This is such an easy dessert that you could each have a different fruit. Try peeled, sliced peaches or a peeled, cored pear. Delightful!

Bread Pudding For Two

Feel like a dish of bread pudding without having it for a week? This is a quick answer for a tasty dessert.

2 slices	bread, buttered and cubed	2
2 tbsp.	sugar	30 mL
1 tbsp.	chopped raisins	15 mL
½ tsp.	grated lemon rind	2 mL
1 tsp.	lemon juice	5 mL
2	eggs	2
½ cup	milk	125 mL
1 tbsp.	sugar	15 mL

1. Combine buttered bread with sugar, raisins, lemon rind and juice. Divide evenly into two custard cups.

2. Separate one egg, saving the white for topping. Beat the whole egg, egg yolk and the milk together. Pour evenly over the bread. Microwave HIGH 2 minutes.

3. Beat egg white until stiff, adding 1 tbsp. of sugar. Pile on top of cooked pudding and microwave 20 seconds on HIGH.

Serves 2.

Peach Upside Down Pudding

¹/₂ cup	flour	125 mL
¹/₄ cup	sugar	60 mL
1 tsp.	baking powder	5 mL
¹/₂ tsp.	salt	2 mL
1 tbsp.	butter or margarine	15 mL
¹/₃ cup	milk	75 mL
1	egg	1
¹/₂ tsp.	vanilla	2 mL
1	peach cut in half	1
2 tbsp.	brown sugar	30 mL
¹/₂ tsp.	cinnamon	2 mL

1. In a medium size mixing bowl combine flour, sugar, baking powder, salt and butter. Mix with an electric mixer until crumbly. Add milk, egg and vanilla. Mix well. Set aside.

2. Place each peach half in the bottom of a dessert bowl. Combine brown sugar and cinnamon and sprinkle half over each peach.

3. Spoon half the batter over each peach. Cover bowls with wax paper and microwave 3–3¹/₂ minutes on MEDIUM power.

Prepare Silky Vanilla Sauce and pour over cooked puddings.

Yields 2 large servings.

Tip
For 4 small servings. Add 1 more peach and divide batter and sauce into 4 equal portions.

Silky Vanilla Sauce

1 tbsp.	cornstarch	15 mL
³/₄ cup	milk	175 mL
2 tbsp.	butter	30 mL
2 tbsp.	powdered sugar	30 mL
1 tsp.	vanilla flavoring	5 mL
pinch	salt	pinch

1. Whisk the above ingredients together in a mixing bowl and micro-wave uncovered on MEDIUM 2–3 minutes or until slightly thickened. Pour over cooked Peach Upside Down Pudding.

Yields ³/₄ cup sauce.

Tropical Baked Bananas

1 tsp.	butter	5 mL
¼ cup	coconut	60 mL
2 tbsp.	butter	30 mL
2	semi ripe bananas	2
¼ cup	brown sugar	60 mL
¼ tsp.	cinnamon	1 mL
¼ tsp.	nutmeg	1 mL
1 tbsp.	rum	15 mL

1. Combine 1 tsp. butter and coconut in small bowl. Microwave uncovered, on HIGH 30–60 seconds or until coconut begins to turn golden brown. Set aside.

2. In a shallow dish, melt 2 tbsp. butter. Peel and slice bananas and coat in melted butter.

3. Combine brown sugar, cinnamon and nutmeg. Coat bananas in sugar mixture. Sprinkle with rum and toasted coconut. Microwave uncovered, on MEDIUM 1½–2½ minutes or until heated through. Spoon into serving dishes, or serve over Old Fashioned Vanilla Ice Cream, page 136.

Apple Crisp For A Pair!

2 tbsp.	quick cooking oats	30 mL
2 tbsp.	brown sugar	30 mL
1 tbsp.	flour	15 mL
1 tbsp.	chopped walnuts	15 mL
pinch	salt	pinch
pinch	cinnamon	pinch
1 tbsp.	butter or margarine	15 mL
1	large apple, peeled, cored and chopped	1

1. In a small bowl, combine oats, sugar, flour, walnuts, salt and cinnamon. Cut in butter and blend until crumbly.

2. Divide apple evenly into two dessert dishes. Sprinkle the oat mixture evenly over each dish.

3. Microwave the two desserts, uncovered on MEDIUM POWER 4½ to 5½ minutes. Serve with ice cream if desired.

BREADS, MUFFINS AND COFFEECAKES

Clockwise from top: —

Honeyed Gingerbread Muffins
Jam Filled Muffins
Shirley's Pumpkin Muffins
Graham Wafer Crumb Muffins
Apricot Fig Loaf
Champagne Jelly
Summer Jam
Peach Orange Marmalade
Cranberry Orange Loaf (toasted)
Colonial Fruit Bread

Soft Ginger Cookies

If you like ginger cookies, these are especially nice microwaved.

2 tbsp.	brown sugar	30 mL
1 cup	flour	250 mL
¼ tsp.	baking soda	1 mL
¼ tsp.	salt	1 mL
½ tsp.	ginger	2 mL
¼ tsp.	each cinnamon and cloves	1 mL
2 tbsp.	butter or margarine	30 mL
2 tbsp.	dark molasses*	30 mL
1	egg	1
2 tbsp.	water	30 mL
½ cup	sugar	125 mL

1. Combine brown sugar, flour, baking soda, salt, ginger, cinnamon and cloves. Add butter and mix with electric mixer until crumbly.

2. In a 1 cup measure, whisk together the molasses, egg and water. Add egg mixture to dry ingredients and stir with a wooden spoon until well blended.

3. Form cookie dough into 12 equal balls. Place the last ½ cup of sugar in a bowl and coat each ball.

4. Place 6 at a time, evenly spaced, on a greased flat dish. Press down slightly with a fork. Do not flatten too much.

5. Microwave uncovered, on MEDIUM POWER 2–2½ minutes or until cookies appear firm. Do not over cook. Remove with spatula immediately. Cool on a wire rack. Repeat with remaining 6 cookies.

Yields 12 cookies.

*To make molasses easier to measure, warm in microwave 20 seconds on HIGH.

Giant Chocolate Chip Cookies For Two

This is the only cookie that won't run out before your cup of tea!

½ cup	butter or margarine	125 mL
1 cup	brown sugar	250 mL
2 tsp.	vanilla	10 mL
1	egg	1
1 cup	flour	250 mL
pinch	salt	pinch
¾ cup	chocolate chips	175 mL

1. In a 4 cup measure, cream butter, sugar and vanilla. Beat in egg. Add flour, salt and chocolate chips. Stir until well combined.

2. Spread half the batter onto a wax paper lined flat dish or an 8 inch casserole cover.

3. Microwave each cookie uncovered, on MEDIUM HIGH 5 to 6 minutes. Turn out onto rack and remove wax paper. Allow to cool completely before eating (10–15 minutes).

Yields 2 large cookies. See photo, page 45.

Ginger Pear Jam

Jams are best made in small quantities in the microwave oven. It takes less than 20 minutes and there will be no scorching of pots! Try interesting variations of your own. A large enough container is necessary to avoid boil-over. Jam, done up in pretty jars, makes a nice gift.

5	pears, peeled, cored and chopped	5
¼ cup	chopped candied ginger	60 mL
1 tsp.	grated lemon rind	5 mL
1¼ cups	sugar	310 mL

1. Combine all ingredients in a 3 qt. (3 L) microwave casserole and microwave on HIGH, covered, 2 minutes.

2. Remove cover and stir fruit. Microwave on HIGH uncovered, 15 to 20 minutes or until jam begins to thicken. Pour into jars and refrigerate.

Yields approximately 1½ cups.

Creamy Butterscotch Pudding

¾ cup	brown sugar	175 mL
¼ cup	butter or margarine	60 mL
3 tbsp.	flour	45 mL
1¼ cups	milk	310 mL
2 tsp.	vanilla	10 mL

1. In a 4 cup measure combine sugar and butter. Microwave uncovered, on HIGH for 1 minute or until the butter has melted.

2. Stir in flour to make a smooth paste. Whisk in milk and vanilla. Microwave uncovered, 3 to 4 minutes or until nicely thickened.

Serves 2.

Tip
For an added treat, sprinkle crushed butterscotch candy on top. See page 133.

Coffee Cheesecake

2 tbsp.	melted butter or margarine	15mL
¼ cup	graham wafer or any cookie crumbs	60 mL
1 tsp.	sugar	5 mL
4 oz.	cream cheese	125 g
1 tbsp.	any coffee liqueur	15 mL
1	egg white, stiffly beaten	1
½ cup	fresh chopped fruit, divided	125 mL

1. In a 1 cup measure melt butter, add crumbs and sugar. Stir until combined. Divide evenly and press crumbs into the bottom of two 6 oz. custard cups.

2. In a separate measure, combine cream cheese and liqueur. Mix with electric mixer until smooth. Fold egg white into cream cheese, divide evenly and pour into two custard cups.

3. Microwave both desserts, uncovered on MEDIUM POWER 2½ to 3 minutes. Top each cheese cake with ¼ cup chopped fruit.

Chocolate Orange Mousse

3 squares	semi sweet chocolate	3
2 tbsp.	Triple Sec, or orange liqueur	30 mL
1/2 tsp.	grated orange rind	2 mL
1/4 cup	sugar	60 mL
2	eggs, separated	2
1/2 cup	whipping cream, whipped	125 mL
	whipped cream and fresh orange slices for garnish	

1. In a 4 cup measure, melt chocolate, uncovered, on MEDIUM 4–5 minutes, stirring every two minutes until melted.

2. In a separate bowl, combine liqueur, orange rind and sugar with egg yolks. Mix well and pour into melted chocolate.

3. Whip egg whites until stiff. Combine with whipped cream and fold into chocolate. Pour into two serving dishes or wine goblets. Garnish with additional whipped cream and orange slices.

Yields 2 cups.

Brandy Alexander Mousse

2 tbsp.	sugar	30 mL
2 tbsp.	cornstarch	30 mL
1 cup	whipping cream, divided	250 mL
1/4 cup	chocolate chips	60 mL
1 tbsp.	coffee liqueur	15 mL
1 tbsp.	sugar	15 mL
1 tbsp.	brandy	15 mL

1. In a 2 cup measure, combine sugar, cornstarch, 1/2 cup whipping cream, chocolate chips and coffee liqueur.

2. Microwave uncovered, on HIGH 1 1/2–2 1/2 minutes or until thickened. Pour into 2 dessert dishes. Cool.

3. Whip remaining 1/2 cup of cream with 1 tbsp. sugar and brandy until still peaks form. Top desserts with whipped cream.

Yields approximately 1 1/2 cups.

Chocolate Mousse

²/₃ cup	milk	150 mL
¹/₂ cup	chocolate chips	125 mL
1	egg	1
1 tbsp.	brandy or any liqueur	15 mL
	whipped cream and chocolate curls for garnish	

1. Microwave milk in a 1 cup measure on HIGH for 1 minute or until hot.

2. Pour milk into a blender and add remaining ingredients one at a time, blending until smooth.

3. Pour into 2 glasses or dessert bowls. Top with whipped cream, chocolate curls or a maraschino cherry if desired.

Chocolate Layer Cake

¹/₄ cup	butter	60 mL
¹/₂ cup	sugar	125 mL
1	egg	1
1 cup	flour	250 mL
¹/₂ tsp.	baking powder	2 mL
¹/₄ tsp.	baking soda	1 mL
pinch	salt	pinch
2–3 tbsp.	cocoa	30 or 45 mL
¹/₂ cup	water	125 mL
¹/₂ tsp.	vanilla	2 mL

1. Combine butter and sugar until smooth. Add egg and beat well.

2. In a separate bowl, blend flour, baking powder, soda, salt and cocoa.

3. Add flour mixture alternately with water and vanilla to the creamed butter. Stir until smooth.

4. Pour batter into a 4 cup (1 L) loaf pan. Cover and microwave on MEDIUM HIGH 3 to 3¹/₂ minutes. Let stand 5 minutes before turning out on rack to cool.

5. Slice cake into two layers. Fill and frost with your favorite icing or with half a recipe of Mocha Seafoam Frosting, page 117.

Yellow Cake

¹/₂ cup	sugar	125 mL
3 tbsp.	butter	45 mL
1	egg	1
1 cup	flour	250 mL
¹/₂ tsp.	baking powder	2 mL
¹/₂ tsp.	baking soda	2 mL
pinch	salt	pinch
¹/₄ cup	milk	60 mL
¹/₂ tsp.	vanilla	2 mL

1. Beat sugar and butter together, add egg. Beat well.

2. Mix flour, baking powder, soda and salt together. Add to the butter mixture alternately with milk and vanilla.

3. Pour batter into a 4 cup (1 L) loaf pan. Cover and microwave on MEDIUM HIGH, 3 to 3¹/₂ minutes. Top with a frosting or sauce of your choice, or use as a base for trifle.

Yields one small cake.

Small Carrot Cake

1 cup	flour	250 mL
³/₄ cup	brown sugar	175 mL
¹/₂ cup	oil	125 mL
2	eggs, beaten	2
¹/₂ tbsp.	cinnamon	7 mL
¹/₂ tsp.	allspice	2 mL
¹/₂ tsp.	ginger	2 mL
1 tsp.	baking soda	5 mL
1 tsp.	baking powder	5 mL
¹/₂ tsp.	salt	2 mL
1 cup	grated carrots	250 mL
¹/₄ cup	chopped raisins	60 mL
	juice and grated rind of half an orange	

1. In a mixing bowl, combine all ingredients in order listed.

2. Pour batter into a 6 cup (1.5 L) ring mold and microwave covered, on HIGH 5 to 6 minutes. Let cool and frost with Orange or Cinnamon Glaze if desired.

Yields one ring.

Orange Glaze

1 cup	sifted powdered sugar	250 mL
¹/₂ tsp.	orange peel	2 mL
1 to 2 tbsp.	hot water	15 to 30 mL

1. Combine all ingredients and mix well. Drizzle over cake.

For **Cinnamon Glaze**, use ¹/₄ tsp. cinnamon in place of orange peel.

Fresh Peach Tarts with Raspberry Sauce

Have some Raspberry Sauce on hand and this colorful dessert can be made at the last minute. Just prepare enough to eat immediately.

6	cooked pastry tart shells	6
2	fresh peaches	2

1. Peel and thinly slice peaches into 6 tart shells. Spoon Raspberry Sauce on top.

Raspberry Sauce

2 cups	fresh or frozen raspberries	500 mL
¹/₃ cup	sugar	75 mL
3 tbsp.	cornstarch	45 mL
2 tsp.	grated orange rind	10 mL
¹/₂ cup	fresh orange juice	125 mL

1. If using frozen raspberries, place in a 4 cup (1 L) mixing bowl and microwave on HIGH 2 to 3 minutes until thawed, stirring once or twice.

2. Combine sugar and cornstarch and mix into raspberries. Microwave on HIGH 2 to 3 minutes, stirring to thoroughly blend.

3. Add orange rind and juice. Microwave on MEDIUM HIGH 2 to 3 minutes until thickened. Strain if desired. Cool. Serve with ice cream, cake, fruit or Sherry Pudding.

See photo, page 27.

Yields about 2 cups of sauce.

Poached Pears in Red Wine Sauce

1 cup	red wine	250 mL
1/2 cup	sugar	125 mL
1/4 tsp.	cinnamon	1 mL
1/4 tsp.	ginger	1 mL
2	fresh pears, peeled and sliced	2
1/2 cup	whipping cream, whipped	125 mL

1. Combine wine, sugar, cinnamon and ginger in a 1 quart measure.

2. Microwave uncovered, on HIGH 8–10 minutes until the wine becomes syrupy.

3. Add sliced pears and microwave an additional 2–3 minutes on HIGH. Allow the pears to cool in the syrup.

4. Serve with whipped cream.

Serves 2 to 4.

Nutmeg Sauce

A truly versatile sauce and so easy to make. Serve it over baked apples, fruit crisps or ice cream.

1 cup	sugar	250 mL
1 tbsp.	flour	15 mL
1 cup	boiling water	250 mL
1 tbsp.	butter	15 mL
1 tsp.	nutmeg	5 mL
1 tbsp.	fresh lemon juice	15 mL

1. Combine sugar and flour in a 4 cup (1 L) mixing bowl.

2. Add boiling water slowly, whisking thoroughly. Microwave on HIGH 2 minutes until slightly thickened, stirring once or twice.

3. Add butter and microwave on MEDIUM HIGH 2 minutes. Stir in nutmeg and lemon juice. Serve warm.

Yields approximately 1 cup.

Variation
For **Peppermint Sauce**, follow the above recipe, replacing nutmeg and lemon juice with 1/4 tsp. peppermint extract and 2 drops of green food coloring. This is attractive served over vanilla ice cream in parfait glasses.

Breads, Muffins and Coffeecakes

Cranberry Orange Bread

Top this with a thin Orange Glaze, or serve toasted with butter, excellent! These small loaves make wonderful gifts for any occasion.

1 cup	sugar	250 mL
¹/₂ tsp.	salt	2 mL
1 tsp.	baking soda	5 mL
1 tsp.	baking powder	5 mL
2 cups	flour	500 mL
2 tbsp.	butter	30 mL
	juice and grated rind of one orange	
1	egg, slightly beaten	1
1 cup	chopped cranberries	250 mL
¹/₂ cup	chopped nuts	125 mL

1. Combine sugar, salt, baking soda, baking powder and flour.

2. In a small measure, combine butter, orange juice and rind. Add enough water to bring to ³/₄ cup liquid. Microwave on HIGH 1 minute.

3. Stir hot liquid into flour mixture and add egg, cranberries and nuts.

4. Spoon half the batter into a small 4 cup microwave loaf pan. Cover and microwave on MEDIUM HIGH 5 to 6 minutes. Remove cover and let stand a few minutes before turning out on rack to cool. Repeat with remaining batter. Top with Thin Orange Glaze (page 17).

Yields 2 small loaves.

See photo, page 9.

Microtip
If using frozen cranberries, do not chop as the juice will discolor the batter.

Quickie Cinnamon Buns

By the time the coffee has perked, these coffee cake type buns will be ready to serve.

1¹/₃ cups	flour	325 mL
2 tsp.	baking powder	10 mL
2 tbsp.	sugar	30 mL
¹/₂ tsp.	salt	2 mL
¹/₄ tsp.	baking soda	1 mL
1	egg, beaten	1
¹/₂ cup	sour cream	125 mL
¹/₄ cup	butter or margarine, softened	60 mL

Cinnamon Spread

¹/₃ cup	soft butter	75 mL
3 tbsp.	brown sugar	45 mL
1 tsp.	cinnamon	5 mL
¹/₂ cup	finely chopped walnuts	125 mL

Syrup

²/₃ cup	butter	150 mL
²/₃ cup	brown sugar	150 mL
¹/₄ cup	currants or chopped raisins	60 mL
¹/₄ cup	chopped cherries, optional	60 mL

1. Mix together, flour, baking powder, sugar, salt and baking soda. Add beaten egg, sour cream and butter. Knead together until a soft dough forms.

2. Roll the dough into a 14″ (35 cm) long by 6″ (15 cm) wide rectangle.

3. Combine butter, brown sugar and cinnamon to a smooth paste. Spread evenly over dough. Sprinkle with chopped nuts.

4. Roll out jelly roll fashion, cut into 14 one inch pieces.

5. In the bottom of a ring mold combine syrup ingredients and microwave on HIGH 1 minute or until butter melts. Stir and pour ¹/₂ the syrup evenly over the bottom of an 8″ (20 cm) ring mold.

6. Place 7 cinnamon buns over syrup. Cover and microwave on MEDIUM HIGH 4 minutes. Let stand 2 minutes before inverting onto serving platter.

7. Repeat with remaining buns and syrup. Serve warm.

Yields 14 buns.

Honeyed Gingerbread Muffins

A hearty muffin, great in texture and appearance.

1¹/₃ cups	all purpose flour	325 mL
¹/₂ tsp.	baking soda	2 mL
¹/₂ tsp.	baking powder	2 mL
¹/₄ tsp.	salt	1 mL
1 tsp.	ground ginger	5 mL
¹/₂ tsp.	cinnamon	2 mL
¹/₄ tsp.	allspice	1 mL
¹/₂ cup	butter or margarine, softened	125 mL
¹/₄ cup	molasses	60 mL
¹/₄ cup	honey	60 mL
¹/₂ cup	warm tap water	125 mL
1	egg	1
¹/₂ cup	shredded unpeeled apple	125 mL

1. Combine all ingredients in a mixing bowl. Beat at medium speed until mixture is well combined.

2. Place only five muffin liners in a microwave muffin ring. Measure ¹/₄ cup batter into each of the 5 liners. Cover and microwave on MEDIUM HIGH 2–2¹/₂ minutes. Repeat with remaining batter.

Serve with Apricot Honey Butter if desired. See page 122.

Yields 10 large muffins.
See photo, page 9.

If honey has crystallized, warm 30 seconds in the microwave.

Molasses will pour easier if warmed 10 or 20 seconds in the microwave while still in its container.

Carrot Muffins

A pleasant change from Carrot Cake. These muffins are good to have on hand for lunches or a picnic. If you do not have a muffin pan see page   for directions.

1¹/₂ cups	finely grated carrots	375 mL
³/₄ cup	vegetable oil	175 mL
¹/₂ cup	brown sugar	125 mL
2	large eggs	2
2 tsp.	vanilla	10 mL
1¹/₄ cups	flour	310 mL
1¹/₂ tsp.	cinnamon	7 mL
¹/₂ tsp.	allspice	2 mL
¹/₂ tsp.	nutmeg	2 mL
1 tsp.	baking powder	5 mL
¹/₂ tsp.	baking soda	2 mL
1 tsp.	salt	5 mL
¹/₄ cup	chopped raisins	60 mL
1 cup	shredded apple	250 mL

1. Place carrots in a small microwave dish. Cover and microwave on HIGH 2 minutes. Set aside.

2. In a large mixing bowl beat together oil, sugar, eggs and vanilla.

3. Combine flour, cinnamon, allspice, nutmeg, baking powder, soda and salt. Add to oil mixture and stir until smooth. Fold in cooked carrots, chopped raisins, and apple.

4. Place 6 large muffin liners into a microwave muffin pan. Spoon approximately ¹/₄ cup batter evenly into liners. Microwave 6 muffins at a time, covered on MEDIUM HIGH, for 2¹/₂ to 3 minutes. Repeat with remaining batter.

Yields 12 muffins.

Top with Cream Cheese Frosting, see page 23. If you're counting calories, remember that cream cheese has HALF the calories of butter.

Cream Cheese Frosting

¹/₂ cup	cream cheese	125 mL
2 tbsp.	butter	30 mL
¹/₄ cup	powdered sugar	60 mL
2 tsp.	lemon juice	10 mL

1. Combine the above ingredients and beat until smooth. Spread over cooled muffins.

Microtip
To soften cream cheese if necessary, remove foil and microwave 10 to 20 seconds on HIGH.

Graham Wafer Crumb Muffins

³/₄ cup	sugar	175 mL
¹/₄ cup	flour	60 mL
1 tsp.	baking powder	5 mL
2 cups	graham wafer crumbs	500 mL
1 cup	dessicated coconut	250 mL
¹/₂ cup	butter	125 mL
1	egg, beaten	1
³/₄ cup	milk	175 mL

1. Combine sugar, flour, baking powder, crumbs and coconut. Cut in butter until mixture is crumbly.

2. Combine beaten egg and milk, add to crumb mixture.

3. With half the batter fill six paper lined muffin cups ³/₄ full. Cover with wax paper and microwave on HIGH 2¹/₂ to 3 minutes. Repeat with remaining batter.

Yields 12 muffins.

See photo, page 9.

Variation
For a crunchy topping, melt 1 tsp. butter in a glass measure. Add ¹/₃ cup coconut, and ¹/₃ cup walnuts. Microwave uncovered, on HIGH 1 to 2 minutes stirring every 30 seconds. Top each muffin with crumb mixture as soon as they are cooked.

Shirley's Pumpkin Muffins

This recipe was shared with us by Joyce's sister, Shirley Kellas, of Winnipeg, Manitoba.

2	eggs	2
1 cup	sugar	250 mL
³/₄ cup	cooking oil	175 mL
1 cup	cooked pumpkin	250 mL
1¹/₂ cups	flour	375 mL
1¹/₂ tsp.	pumpkin pie spice*	7 mL
1 tsp.	baking powder	5 mL
¹/₂ tsp.	salt	2 mL
¹/₂ cup	chopped raisins	125 mL
¹/₂ cup	chopped walnuts	125 mL

1. In a large mixing bowl, beat together, eggs, sugar, oil and pumpkin.

2. In a separate bowl, combine flour, pumpkin spice, baking powder and salt. Add to pumpkin mixture, blending thoroughly. Fold in raisins and walnuts.

3. Place 6 large muffin liners into a microwave muffin ring and fill ³/₄ full of batter. Cover and microwave on HIGH 3 to 3¹/₂ minutes. Repeat with remaining batter.

Yields 12 large muffins.

See photo, page 9.

*Pumpkin Pie Spice
Thoroughly mix together 1 tablespoon EACH of the following: allspice, cinnamon, cloves, ginger and nutmeg. Store in a tightly sealed container.

Bran Muffins

1 cup	flour	250 mL
1/2 cup	brown sugar	125 mL
1/2 tsp.	salt	2 mL
1/2 tsp.	soda	2 mL
2 tsp.	baking powder	10 mL
1 1/2 cups	bran	375 mL
2/3 cup	chopped raisins	150 mL
1 cup	sour milk	250 mL
2 tbsp.	molasses	30 mL
1	egg, slightly beaten	1
2 tbsp.	butter, melted	30 mL

1. Combine all ingredients in a mixing bowl in order listed. Mix thoroughly.

2. Line a microwave muffin pan with paper liners. Fill each muffin cup 2/3 full. Cover and microwave on MEDIUM 5 minutes, for 6 muffins. Repeat with remaining batter.

Yields 12 muffins.

Microtip
In place of sour milk, use whole milk plus 1 tbsp. lemon juice or vinegar. Allow to stand 1 or 2 minutes.

Cover muffin pan with an inverted pie plate or cake pan.

Chopped raisins give more flavor than whole raisins.

Sugar 'n' Spice Coffee Cake

This rich coffee cake can be ready in minutes. A special treat for your next coffee break.

Cake Batter

1¼ cups	flour	310 mL
2 tsp.	baking powder	10 mL
¼ tsp.	salt	1 mL
¼ cup	butter or margarine, firm	60 mL
½ cup	sugar	125 mL
1	egg, beaten	1
⅓ cup	milk	75 mL
2 tsp.	vanilla flavoring	10 mL

Topping

¼ cup	flour	60 mL
2 tbsp.	brown sugar	30 mL
1 tsp.	cinnamon	5 mL
¼ tsp.	allspice	1 mL
½ cup	chopped walnuts	125 mL
¼ cup	coconut, optional	60 mL
¼ cup	butter or margarine, firm	60 mL

1. Combine flour, baking powder, and salt. With electric mixer beat in butter, sugar, egg, milk, and vanilla. Place batter in an 8" (20 cm) ring mold.

2. Combine all topping ingredients, blending in butter until crumbly. Sprinkle topping over batter.

3. Cover with wax paper, microwave on MEDIUM HIGH 5–6 minutes.

CAKES

Top — Orange Coconut Cake
Center — Great Grandma's Sheepwagon Carrot Cake
Bottom — Leanne's Chocolate Chip Pumpkin Loaf

Fruit Topped Coffee Cake

Use any fruit you like for this. Chopped cranberries make a colorful, tangy topping.

1¼ cups	flour	310 mL
½ cup	sugar	125 mL
1 tsp.	baking powder	5 mL
½ tsp.	baking soda	2 mL
¼ tsp.	salt	1 mL
¼ cup	butter	60 mL
1	egg	1
3 tbsp.	orange juice	45 mL
1 tbsp.	water	15 mL
1½ cups	chopped cranberries, fresh or frozen	375 mL

Topping

⅓ cup	flour	75 mL
½ cup	brown sugar	125 mL
½ tsp.	cinnamon	2 mL
¼ cup	butter	60 mL

1. In a mixing bowl, combine flour, sugar, baking powder, soda and salt. Cut in butter until crumbly.

2. In a separate container, beat the egg, add orange juice and water. Blend into dry ingredients.

3. Spoon batter into a 6 cup (1.5 L) ring mold. Spoon chopped (thawed) cranberries over top.

4. Mix together topping ingredients and sprinkle over cranberries. Microwave 7 to 8 minutes on MEDIUM HIGH.

Hawaiian Coffee Cake

Coconut and macadamia nuts give this a real Hawaiian flair.

³/₄ cup	sugar	175 mL
¹/₂ cup	soft butter or margarine	125 mL
2	eggs	2
1 cup	sour cream	250 mL
1 tsp.	vanilla	5 mL
2 cups	flour	500 mL
1 tsp.	allspice or cinnamon	5 mL
1 tsp.	baking powder	5 mL
1 tsp.	baking soda	5 mL
pinch	salt	pinch
¹/₂ cup	chopped macadamia nuts	125 mL
¹/₂ cup	medium coconut, toasted*	125 mL
¹/₄ cup	brown sugar	60 mL
1 tsp.	cinnamon	5 mL
1 tbsp.	grated lemon or orange rind	15 mL

1. Combine sugar, butter and eggs in a large bowl and mix with electric mixer until creamy. Add sour cream and vanilla.

2. Sift together flour, allspice, baking powder, soda and salt. Add nuts and combine with sour cream mixture.

3. In a separate bowl combine coconut, brown sugar, cinnamon and rind. Sprinkle in the bottom of a 12 cup, microwave bundt pan, or ring mold.

4. Pour batter evenly over coconut mixture. Cover loosely with wax paper and microwave on MEDIUM, 6–8 minutes.

Optional
Drizzle with **Coconut Frosting** Page 115.

Microtip
Toast ¹/₂ cup of coconut with 1 tsp. butter in a 2 cup measure on HIGH for 1–1¹/₂ minutes, or until coconut just begins to turn golden brown. Stir every 30 seconds. Watch carefully as coconut browns quickly.

Orange Walnut Coffee Cake

Orange Coating

2 tbsp.	butter	30 mL
2 tbsp.	finely grated orange rind	30 mL
3 tbsp.	sugar	45 mL
1/3 cup	finely chopped walnuts	75 mL

Coffee Cake

1 1/2 cups	flour	375 mL
1 tbsp.	baking powder	15 mL
1/4 tsp.	salt	1 mL
1/3 cup	sugar	75 mL
2	eggs, beaten	2
1/2 cup	milk	125 mL
1/4 cup	oil	60 mL

Orange Coating

1. Melt butter in a 6 cup ring mold, coating sides and bottom well.

2. Blend orange rind, sugar and walnuts together. Press onto bottom and sides of ring mold. Set aside.

Coffee Cake

1. Mix together, flour, baking powder, salt and sugar. Add eggs, milk and oil. Combine thoroughly.

2. Spoon cake batter evenly over orange nut mixture.

3. Cover and microwave on HIGH 3 1/2 to 4 minutes. Let stand 5 minutes.

4. Invert on serving plate and serve warm with butter. Have a friend in for coffee and enjoy!

Kitchen Tip

If you have a food processor, place the orange peel, sugar and walnuts into the bowl with metal blade inserted. Process a few seconds for the right grind.

Frozen Blueberry Johnny Cake

Adding frozen blueberries gives a new twist to an old favorite. A nice change to serve for Sunday Brunch.

1 cup	milk	250 mL
1 tbsp.	lemon juice	15 mL
1 tsp.	baking soda	5 mL
1/2 tsp.	cream of tartar	2 mL
1/2 cup	sugar	125 mL
1 cup	corn meal	250 mL
1 cup	flour	250 mL
1/4 cup	margarine	60 mL
1	egg, beaten	1
1/2 cup	frozen blueberries	125 mL

1. In a 2 cup measure combine milk, lemon juice, baking soda and cream of tartar. Stir and set aside.

2. In a mixing bowl combine sugar, corn meal and flour. Cut in butter with a pastry blender or electric mixer until crumbly. Add milk, beaten egg and blueberries. Stir until smooth.

3. Pour batter into an 8" (20 cm) microwave ring mold, cover with wax paper. Microwave on MEDIUM HIGH 5–6 minutes. Cool before removing from pan. Enjoy!

Variation
Johnny Cake
Johnny Cake is also nice served warm for breakfast, with maple syrup. Follow above directions for Blueberry Johnny Cake omitting 1/2 cup flour and the blueberries.

Microwave 1 small package of jelly powder and 1 cup tap water on HIGH 3–4 minutes. Stir to dissolve. This eliminates pre boiling the water. Follow package directions after dissolving.

Cakes

Apple Walnut Spice Cake

¹/₄ cup	margarine	60 mL
³/₄ cup	brown sugar	175 mL
1	egg	1
1¹/₄ cups	flour	310 mL
¹/₂ tsp.	baking powder	2 mL
1 tsp.	baking soda	5 mL
¹/₄ tsp.	salt	1 mL
1 tsp.	cinnamon	5 mL
¹/₄ tsp.	cloves or allspice	1 mL
¹/₄ tsp.	nutmeg	1 mL
1	apple, peeled and grated	1
2 tbsp.	water	30 mL
¹/₄ cup	chopped walnuts	60 mL

1. Cream margarine and sugar together. Add egg and beat until light and fluffy.

2. In a separate bowl, combine flour, baking powder, soda, salt, cinnamon, cloves or allspice and nutmeg.

3. Add dry ingredients to butter mixture alternately with apples and water. Fold in walnuts.

4. Spoon batter into an 8" (20 cm) round microwave cake pan. Cover and microwave on HIGH 3¹/₂ to 4¹/₂ minutes. Cool before frosting with Coffee Seafoam Frosting (page 117).

Yields 1 — 8" cake.

Great Grandma's Sheepwagon Carrot Cake

In the days of the covered wagons, eggs and oil were not always available. With no eggs and oil used, the secret to this recipe is in the precooking of the carrots, raisins and spices.

1¹/₃ cups	white sugar	325 mL
1¹/₃ cups	water	325 mL
1 cup	raisins	250 mL
1 tbsp.	butter	15 mL
3 cups	finely grated carrots	750 mL
1 tsp.	cinnamon	5 mL
¹/₂ tsp.	cloves	2 mL
1 tsp.	nutmeg	5 mL

1. Combine all the above ingredients in a large cooking bowl and microwave on HIGH covered, 7 minutes, until mixture comes to a boil. Stir. Microwave on MEDIUM HIGH for 3 to 4 minutes. Set aside.

1 cup	chopped walnuts	250 mL
2¹/₂ cups	sifted flour	625 mL
¹/₂ tsp.	salt	2 mL
1 tsp.	soda	5 mL
2 tsp.	baking powder	10 mL

1. Combine above ingredients and blend thoroughly with the carrot mixture.

2. Spoon mixture into a large 12 cup (3 L) microwave bundt pan. Cover and microwave on MEDIUM HIGH 10 minutes. Remove cover and microwave another 4 to 6 minutes. Let stand 20 minutes before turning out. This cake is delicious as is or try a slice buttered. Frost with a Cream Cheese Frosting if desired. See page 35.

See photo, page 28.

Cream Cheese Frosting

4 oz.	cream cheese	125 g
2 tbsp.	butter	30 mL
1/2 tsp.	vanilla	2 mL
1/2 cup	powdered sugar	125 mL
few drops	milk	few drops
1/4 cup	ground walnuts	60 mL

1. In a mixing bowl, soften cheese and butter 5 or 10 seconds on HIGH. Beat together with vanilla and powdered sugar. Add a few drops of milk to thin frosting if necessary. Drizzle over cooled cake. Sprinkle with ground walnuts.

Granola Carrot Cake

A wholesome nutritious combination, you will be sure to like.

2 cups	grated carrots	500 mL
1/2 cup	brown sugar	125 mL
1 1/4 cups	flour	310 mL
1 tsp.	baking powder	5 mL
1/2 tsp.	salt	2 mL
1/2 tsp.	cinnamon	2 mL
1/2 tsp.	allspice	2 mL
1/4 cup	margarine	60 mL
1 cup	granola	250 mL
2	eggs	2
1/4 cup	warm water	60 mL

1. Place carrots in a 2 cup measure and microwave, covered, on HIGH 2–3 minutes. Keep covered and set aside.

2. In a mixing bowl combine brown sugar, flour, baking powder, salt, cinnamon and allspice. Cut butter into flour mixture. Mix with electric beater until crumbly. Stir in granola.

3. Beat eggs with warm water and add to dry ingredients.

4. Spread batter evenly into an 8" (20 cm) ring mold. Cover with wax paper and microwave on MEDIUM 6–7 minutes. Cool 5 minutes before turning out.

Frost with Cream Cheese (page 23) or Creamy Orange Frosting (page 117) if desired.

Pineapple Cake

Dress up a cake mix with pineapple and a crunchy topping.

1 – 8 oz.	single layer white cake mix	227 gr.
1	egg	1
½ tsp.	vanilla flavoring	2 mL
½ cup	crushed, undrained pineapple	125 mL
½ cup	crushed corn flakes	125 mL
½ cup	toasted coconut	125 mL

1. Combine dry cake mix with egg, vanilla and crushed pineapple. Beat for 2 minutes.

2. Pour batter into an 8 inch (20 cm) straight sided cake pan.

3. Combine corn flakes and coconut and sprinkle evenly over batter. Microwave covered, on HIGH 3½–4 minutes.

Banana Oatmeal Snackin' Cake

Not a cake, not a brownie. Try It, You'll Like It!

1 cup	quick cooking oats	250 mL
¾ cup	flour	175 mL
¼ tsp.	salt	1 mL
¾ cup	brown sugar	175 mL
½ cup	butter or margarine	125 mL
1 tsp.	vanilla	5 mL
¾ cup	mashed banana	175 mL
1	egg	1

1. Combine oats, flour, salt and sugar. With electric mixer blend in butter until mixture resembles a coarse meal.

2. In a separate bowl, combine vanilla, banana and egg. Add to dry ingredients and combine thoroughly.

3. Spread batter into a 9″ (23 cm) cake or quiche pan. Microwave uncovered on MEDIUM HIGH for 3½ to 4 minutes. Serve warm, with a glass of cold milk to a couple of hungry kids.

Banana Cake

1 cup	flour	250 mL
1/2 cup	sugar	125 mL
1 tbsp.	baking powder	15 mL
1/2 tsp.	salt	2 mL
2 tbsp.	margarine	30 mL
1/4 cup	milk	60 mL
1	mashed banana*	1
1	egg	1
1/4 cup	chopped walnuts	60 mL

1. Combine flour, sugar, baking powder and salt in a mixing bowl. Cut in margarine until crumbly.

2. *Reserve 2 tbsp. mashed banana for frosting. Add remaining mashed banana, milk and egg to flour mixture, combine thoroughly. Add walnuts.

3. Pour into an 8" (20 cm) round microwave cake pan. Cover and microwave on MEDIUM 5 to 6 minutes or until completely cooked.

Microtip
If cake does not cook in the center, shield cooked portion with aluminum foil and microwave on HIGH 1 minute.

Banana Frosting

2 tbsp.	margarine, softened*	30 mL
2 tbsp.	mashed banana	30 mL
1 tsp.	lemon juice	5 mL
1/2 cup	powdered sugar	125 mL
1/4 cup	finely chopped walnuts	60 mL

1. In a small bowl, beat margarine and banana until smooth.

2. Add lemon juice and powdered sugar. Mix until smooth. Spread on cooled cake. Garnish with walnuts.

*Soften margarine in microwave 10 to 20 seconds on HIGH. Do not melt.

Pineapple Topped Cake

A very colorful attractive dessert.

Cake Layer

½ cup	flour	125 mL
¼ cup	sugar	60 mL
1½ tsp.	baking powder	7 mL
½ tsp.	salt	2 mL
1 tbsp.	butter or margarine	15 mL
⅓ cup	milk	75 mL
1	egg	1
½ tsp.	almond flavoring	2 mL

1. In a large mixing bowl, combine flour, sugar, baking powder and salt.

2. Cut in butter until crumbly. Add milk, egg, almond flavoring and beat well.

3. Pour batter into a round 9″ (23 cm) cake or quiche pan. Cover and microwave on HIGH 2–2½ minutes. Remove cover and set aside.

Fruit Topping

14 oz. can	crushed pineapple	398 mL
¼ cup	sugar	60 mL
2 tbsp.	cornstarch	30 mL
½ cup	chopped maraschino cherries, drained	125 mL

1. In a glass mixing bowl, combine pineapple, sugar and cornstarch. Microwave uncovered, on HIGH 5 to 6 minutes, until thickened, stirring once or twice during cooking.

2. Add drained maraschino cherries to thickened pineapple. Pour over cooked cake.

Meringue Topping

2	egg whites	2
2 tbsp.	sugar	30 mL
¼ tsp.	almond flavoring	1 mL
	toasted coconut for garnish	

1. Beat egg whites until frothy. Add sugar and almond flavoring and beat until stiff.

2. Spread meringue on top of fruit and microwave, uncovered, on HIGH 1 minute. Decorate with toasted coconut.

Cinnamon Bundt Cake

The cinnamon gives a unique flavor to this pound cake.

Crumb Mixture

2¼ cups	flour	560 mL
¾ cup	sugar	175 mL
3 tbsp.	cinnamon	45 mL
¾ cup	margarine or butter	175 mL
¼ cup	chopped nuts	60 mL

Batter

1	egg	1
1 cup	milk	250 mL
1 tbsp.	lemon juice	15 mL
1 tsp.	baking soda	5 mL
½ tsp.	baking powder	2 mL
2 tsp.	vanilla	10 mL
½ cup	chopped raisins	125 mL

1. For crumb mixture, combine flour, sugar and cinnamon. Cut in butter and mix with electric mixer or pastry blender until crumbly. Stir in nuts. Set aside.

2. In a large bowl beat egg, add milk, lemon juice, baking soda, baking powder, vanilla and raisins. Add crumb mixture and stir until smooth. Batter will be fairly thick.

3. Pour batter into a greased 12 cup microwave bundt pan. Cover with waxed paper and microwave on MEDIUM HIGH 7–9 minutes or until toothpick inserted in cake comes out clean. Drizzle with Cinnamon Glaze, (page 17).

Cinnamon is the most important baking spice, distinctively sweet, mildly pungent and spicy.

Gingercake

½ cup	brown sugar	125 mL
¼ cup	butter, chilled	60 mL
1½ cups	flour	375 mL
1 tsp.	baking powder	5 mL
½ tsp.	baking soda	2 mL
2 tsp.	ginger	10 mL
1 tsp.	cinnamon	5 mL
½ tsp.	salt	2 mL
⅓ cup	molasses	75 mL
2	eggs	2
⅓ cup	hot tap water	75 mL

1. Combine brown sugar, butter, flour, baking powder, soda, ginger, cinnamon and salt in a large mixing bowl. Mix with electric mixer until ingredients resemble cornmeal.

2. In a separate bowl, combine molasses with hot water and whisk in eggs, one at a time, beating after each addition.

3. Blend dry ingredients together with liquid ingredients and beat until well combined.

4. Pour into an 8" (20 cm) microwave cake pan. Cover and microwave on MEDIUM 6 to 7 minutes. Cool and serve with Apple Snow, page 98.

Ginger Cake Variations
Carrot Gingercake with Lemon Sauce
Follow the above recipe, add ½ cup finely grated raw carrot to the dry ingredients. See page 92 for Lemon Sauce.

Orange Gingercake With Ginger Cream
Follow the above recipe substituting the hot water for hot reconstituted orange juice. Add 1 tsp. grated orange rind and 1 tsp. instant coffee granules. Frost with Orange Cream on page 41.

Moist Ginger Date Cake

The dates add moisture and flavour to this cake. Even better the next day!

1 cup	dates	250 mL
²/₃ cup	water	150 mL
1 tsp.	baking soda	5 mL
¹/₂ cup	butter	125 mL
¹/₂ cup	brown sugar	125 mL
3 tbsp.	molasses	45 mL
1 tbsp.	corn syrup	15 mL
2	eggs	2
1 cup	flour	250 mL
2 tsp.	ground ginger	10 mL
2 tbsp.	powdered sugar	30 mL

1. Combine dates and water into a 4 cup glass measure. Microwave uncovered, on HIGH 2 to 3 minutes, or until completely softened, stirring often. Add baking soda. Set aside.

2. Cream butter, brown sugar, molasses and corn syrup together. Beat in eggs, one at a time.

3. Combine flour with ginger and add alternately with dates to creamed mixture.

4. Pour batter into a 9" (23 cm) round microwave cake or quiche pan and microwave covered, on MEDIUM HIGH 5 to 7 minutes. Cool. Sprinkle with 2 tbsp. powdered sugar.

Tip
To sprinkle powdered sugar in a pretty pattern on top of the cake, place a small doily on top and sprinkle sugar over it.

Orange Cream Frosting

1 cup	whipping cream	250 mL
1 tbsp.	powdered sugar	15 mL
¹/₄ tsp.	ginger	1 mL
¹/₂ tsp.	grated orange peel	2 mL

1. Whip cream until thickened, add remaining ingredients and beat until stiff peaks form.

Laisy Daisy Cake

This is an old favorite, sometimes called Hot Milk Cake.

2	eggs	2
³/₄ cup	sugar	175 mL
¹/₂ cup	milk	125 mL
1 tbsp.	margarine or butter	15 mL
1 cup	flour	250 mL
1 tsp.	baking powder	5 mL
¹/₂ tsp.	salt	2 mL

1. In a large mixing bowl combine eggs and sugar. Set aside.

2. In a 2 cup measure combine milk and margarine. Microwave uncovered, on HIGH 1–2 minutes or long enough to scald the milk.*

3. Combine flour, baking powder and salt. Blend hot milk alternately with flour into egg mixture.

4. Pour into an 8″ (20 cm) round cake pan. Microwave, covered, on HIGH 3–4 minutes.

Frost with Brown Sugar Frosting.

*Scald means to just bring to the boil.

Brown Sugar Frosting

1 cup	brown sugar	250 mL
¹/₃ cup	butter or margarine	75 mL
¹/₃ cup	milk	75 mL
¹/₂ cup	coconut	125 mL

1. Combine all ingredients in a mixing bowl. Microwave on HIGH uncovered 2 to 3 minutes until the sugar is dissolved.

Lemon Walnut Cake

1 cup	sugar	250 mL
1 tbsp.	grated lemon rind	15 mL
1¹/₂ cups	flour	375 mL
1 tsp.	baking powder	5 mL
¹/₄ tsp.	salt	1 mL
¹/₂ cup	butter or margarine	125 mL
¹/₃ cup	milk	75 mL
2 tbsp.	lemon juice	30 mL
2	eggs	2
¹/₃ cup	chopped walnuts	75 mL

1. Combine sugar, lemon rind, flour, baking powder and salt. Stir until blended.

2. Cut butter into dry ingredients and mix with electric mixer until crumbly.

3. In a 1 cup measure beat together milk, eggs and lemon juice. Add to dry ingredients. Fold in walnuts.

4. Pour into an 8″ (20 cm) microwave ring mold, cover with wax paper and microwave on MEDIUM HIGH 6–7 minutes. Cool and frost with Lemon Butter Cream (page 147).

To extract juice from lemons, limes, oranges or grapefruit, place in the microwave for 15 to 20 seconds.

Orange Coconut Cake

¼ cup	margarine	60 mL
¾ cup	sugar	175 mL
1	egg	1
1 cup	flour	250 mL
1 tsp.	baking powder	5 mL
½ tsp.	baking soda	2 mL
¼ tsp.	salt	1 mL
½ cup	hot tap water	125 mL
2 tbsp.	frozen orange juice concentrate	30 mL
1 tbsp.	freshly grated orange rind	15 mL
½ cup	shredded coconut	125 mL
	shredded coconut, for garnish	

1. Beat margarine and sugar until light and fluffy. Add egg and beat well.

2. In a separate measure, combine flour, baking powder, soda and salt.

3. In another bowl, combine water, orange concentrate and rind.

4. Blend dry ingredients alternately with liquid ingredients into the butter mixture. Add coconut and combine well. Let batter stand 10 minutes. This will produce a lighter cake.

5. Spoon batter evenly into an 8" (20 cm) round microwave cake pan. Cover and microwave on HIGH 3 to 4 minutes. Let cake cool. Frost with Apricot Honey Seafoam Frosting, Page 116 or Creamy Orange Icing, Page 117. Sprinkle with coconut.

See photo, page 27.

Microtip
If your oven has a tendency to undercook cakes in the center, we suggest you try elevating the cake dish on a soup bowl, right side up. Microwave on a Medium power setting for 7 to 8 minutes.

Variation
For plain **Vanilla Cake**, omit orange juice concentrate, orange rind and coconut, and add 2 tsp. vanilla.

For a layer cake, double the recipe and bake half the batter at a time. Fill and frost with your favorite Seafoam Frosting.

BARS, SLICES AND SQUARES

Top Dish Clockwise

Sugared Orange Peel dipped in Chocolate
Butterscotch Candy
Chocolate Rum Truffles — Coconut and Sugar Coated
Penuche Fudge
Almond Butter Crunch

Giant Chocolate Chip Cookie

Oval Plate Clockwise:

Dream Squares
Thimble Cookies
Oatmeal Fingers dipped in Chocolate
Coconut Topped Raisin Bars
Gambier Bars
Butterscotch Brownies

Dark Chocolate Layer Cake

The ultimate for chocolate lovers!

³/₄ cup	margarine, softened	175 mL
1³/₄ cups	sugar	425 mL
2	eggs, beaten	2
1¹/₃ cups	warm tap water	325 mL
2 tsp.	vanilla	10 mL
2 cups	flour	500 mL
¹/₂ tsp.	salt	2 mL
1 tsp.	baking powder	5 mL
1 tsp.	baking soda	5 mL
³/₄ cup	cocoa	175 mL

1. Cream margarine and sugar together, add eggs and beat until fluffy. Add warm water and vanilla.

2. In a large bowl, combine flour, salt, baking powder, soda, and cocoa. Add flour to liquid ingredients and beat for two minutes on medium speed.

3. Pour HALF the batter into a wax paper lined 9″ (23 cm) round microwave cake or quiche pan.

4. Microwave covered, 4 to 5¹/₂ minutes on MEDIUM HIGH. Set on rack to cool. Repeat with second layer.

Frost with Creole Frosting page 115.

Tip — For an elegant 3 layer cake, divide batter equally into 3 parts and microwave, each layer covered, on MEDIUM HIGH 2 to 3 minutes.

Lining the cake pan with wax paper enables you to remove the cake almost immediately after cooking.

Mary's Butterfly Cupcakes

Susan's Mom made these frequently for her family. They are so quick and easy to make with the help of the microwave.

Creamy Lemon Filling

½ cup	sugar	125 mL
2 tbsp.	cornstarch	30 mL
dash	salt	dash
1 cup	water	250 mL
1	egg yolk, beaten	1
2 tbsp.	butter or margarine	30 mL
2 tbsp.	lemon juice	30 mL
1 tsp.	grated lemon rind (optional)	5 mL

1. Combine sugar, cornstarch and salt. Whisk in water, egg yolk, butter, lemon juice and rind. Microwave uncovered, on HIGH 4–5 minutes or until thickened, stirring often. Refrigerate until completely cooled.

Cake Batter

1 – 8 oz.	single yellow cake mix	250 g
	powdered sugar	

1. Combine cake mix according to package directions. Beat until smooth. Batter will be easier to pour from a large measuring cup or pouring pitcher.

2. Place six muffin liners in microwave muffin ring. Fill each cupcake half full of batter. Cover and microwave on MEDIUM HIGH 2 to 2½ minutes. Repeat with remaining batter.

3. Cool cupcakes completely and slice ¼" (.5 cm) off the top. Top each cupcake with ½ tbsp. lemon filling. Cut the sliced portion into two and place in a butterfly fashion on top of the cupcake. Sprinkle with powdered sugar.

Yields 12 muffins.

Diet Cola Cupcakes

Some diet!

½ cup	milk	125 mL
2 tsp.	lemon juice	10 mL
¼ tsp.	baking soda	1 mL
¼ cup	butter	60 mL
¼ cup	vegetable oil	60 mL
2 tbsp.	cocoa	30 mL
½ cup	diet cola	125 mL
¾ cup	mini marshmallows	175 mL
½ cup	sugar	125 mL
¼ tsp.	salt	1 mL
1½ cups	flour	375 mL
1	egg, beaten	1
1 tsp.	vanilla	5 mL

1. Combine milk, lemon juice and soda in a 1 cup measure and set aside to sour.

2. In a separate bowl combine butter, vegetable oil, cocoa, diet cola and marshmallows. Microwave uncovered, on HIGH 2–2½ minutes or until boiling, stirring once.

3. In a separate bowl combine sugar, salt and flour, add to cola mixture. Add sour milk, egg and vanilla and blend thoroughly.

4. Line a microwave muffin pan with 6 paper liners. Pour ¼ cup batter into each liner. Microwave, 6 at a time, uncovered on HIGH 2½ to 3 minutes. Repeat with remaining batter. One cupcake takes approximately 30 seconds.

Diet Cola Frosting

¼ cup	butter	60 mL
¼ cup	diet cola	60 mL
3 tbsp.	cocoa	45 mL
1½ cups	icing sugar	375 mL

1. In an 8 cup measure combine butter and diet cola. Microwave uncovered on HIGH for 1½–2 minutes until boiling. Add cocoa and icing sugar.

2. Allow to cool in refrigerator for 5 minutes. Spread over cupcakes.

Pumpkin Loaf

Flavor improves after being stored for 24 hours.

³/₄ cup	sugar	175 mL
¹/₂ tsp.	cloves	2 mL
¹/₂ tsp.	cinnamon	2 mL
¹/₂ tsp.	nutmeg	2 mL
¹/₂ tsp.	ginger	2 mL
¹/₂ tsp.	baking powder	2 mL
¹/₂ tsp.	baking soda	2 mL
1²/₃ cup	flour	400 mL
¹/₂ tsp.	grated orange rind	2 mL
¹/₃ cup	chopped raisins	75 mL
1 cup	canned pumpkin	250 mL
¹/₄ cup	vegetable oil	60 mL
2	eggs	2
¹/₄ cup	orange juice	60 mL

1. Combine sugar, cloves, cinnamon, nutmeg, ginger, baking powder, baking soda, flour, orange rind and raisins.

2. In a separate bowl combine pumpkin, oil, eggs and orange juice. Beat until smooth. Add to dry ingredients and blend well.

3. Pour batter into an 8″ (20 cm) microwave ring mold. Cover with wax paper and microwave on MEDIUM HIGH 6 to 7 minutes. Cool and store in an air tight container.

Baking In A Loaf Pan
If you have a microwave loaf pan with a cover you can successfully bake a loaf. Follow steps one and two. Leave batter in bowl and microwave on MEDIUM HIGH for 2 minutes, uncovered, stirring after each minute. When batter has warmed, pour it into the loaf pan. Cover and microwave on MEDIUM HIGH for 7 to 8 minutes. Allow to cool 10 minutes before removing from the pan.

Variation
Leanne's Chocolate Chip Pumpkin Loaf
This is an unusual but very tasty and colorful combination.
Follow the above directions, substituting ¹/₂ cup chocolate chips for the raisins.

See photo, page 27.

Date Nut Ring Loaf

This was a family favorite years ago which took about an hour to bake. Oh, to have a microwave in those days!

1 cup	pitted chopped dates	250 mL
1 cup	boiling water	250 mL
¹/₂ cup	chopped walnuts	125 mL
1 tsp.	baking soda	5 mL
1 tbsp.	butter	15 mL
1	egg	1
1 cup	sugar	250 mL
1 tbsp.	vanilla	15 mL
1¹/₂ cups	flour	375 mL
¹/₂ tsp.	salt	2 mL

1. Combine dates and water. Microwave on HIGH 4 to 5 minutes. Add chopped walnuts and sprinkle with baking soda. Set aside.

2. In a separate bowl, beat the butter, egg, sugar and vanilla together.

3. Combine flour and salt into the butter mixture alternately with the dates.

4. Spoon batter into a 6 cup (1.5 L) ring mold. Cover and microwave MEDIUM HIGH, 5 to 6 minutes. Remove cover and microwave 2 to 3 more minutes. When cool, frost with a thin butter icing if desired.

Yields one ring.

Variation
Instead of mixing walnuts with the dates, use them as a topping. Sprinkle walnuts on top of the ring for the last 2 or 3 minutes of cooking.

Drizzle a mixture of 1 tsp. rum with 1 tbsp. water on top of ring while still warm.

Peanut Butter Cake

A delicate taste of peanut butter in both the cake and icing.

⅓ cup	butter or margarine	75 mL
¾ cup	brown sugar	175 mL
¼ cup	smooth peanut butter	60 mL
1 tsp.	vanilla	5 mL
2	eggs	2
1½ cups	flour	375 mL
1 tsp.	baking powder	5 mL
½ tsp.	baking soda	2 mL
½ cup	warm tap water	125 mL

1. Cream butter and sugar together. Add peanut butter, vanilla and eggs, beat well.

2. Combine flour, baking powder and soda. Add alternately with water to butter mixture, blending thoroughly after each addition.

3. Line an 8″ round (20 cm) 2″ (5 cm) deep, cake pan with wax paper. Pour batter into pan and microwave on HIGH 4 to 4½ minutes. Let cool in pan 5 minutes before turning out. Ice with Peanut Butter Icing.

Peanut Butter Icing

3 tbsp.	butter or margarine	45 mL
3 tbsp.	smooth peanut butter	45 mL
1 tsp.	vanilla	5 mL
2 cups	sifted powdered sugar	500 mL
2 or 3 tbsp.	milk	30 or 45 mL
	chopped peanuts	

1. Cream butter, peanut butter and vanilla together. Beat in sugar alternately with enough milk to make light and fluffy.

2. Sprinkle with chopped peanuts.

Yields enough to frost top and sides of one cake.

Microtip
If you wish to leave the cake in pan, do not use the wax paper.

For a Peanut Butter layer cake, microwave half the batter at a time 2½ to 3 minutes on HIGH. Fill and frost with Peanut Butter Icing. Drizzle Chocolate Glaze in a criss cross fashion over icing if desired. Top with chopped peanuts.

Chocolate Glaze

1 tbsp.	BOILING water	15 mL
2 tbsp.	chocolate chips	30 mL

1. Stir chocolate chips into boiling water until smooth.

Chocolate Almond Snackin' Cake

Better than the packaged snackin' cakes and no additives!

½ cup	brown sugar	125 mL
¼ cup	white sugar	60 mL
¼ cup	margarine	60 mL
2	eggs	2
½ tsp.	almond extract	2 mL
1 tsp.	baking powder	5 mL
½ cup	flour	125 mL
pinch	salt	pinch
2 tbsp.	cocoa	30 mL
⅓ cup	finely chopped walnuts	75 mL

1. Combine brown sugar, white sugar and margarine with electric mixer. Add eggs and almond extract.

2. Gradually beat in baking powder, flour, salt and cocoa until smooth. Fold in nuts.

3. Place batter in an 8″ (20 cm) microwave cake pan. Cover and microwave on MEDIUM HIGH 4 to 4½ minutes. Allow to cool and then cut into squares.

Beer Fruit Cake

This recipe is bound to create a new interest for men in the kitchen.

1¹/₂ cups	flour	375 mL
1 tsp.	baking powder	5 mL
¹/₂ tsp.	salt	2 mL
³/₄ cup	brown sugar	175 mL
1 tsp.	cinnamon	5 mL
¹/₂ tsp.	ginger	2 mL
¹/₂ tsp.	nutmeg	2 mL
¹/₄ cup	margarine	60 mL
1 – 6 pack	beer, divided*	
1	egg, well beaten	1
¹/₄ cup	chopped walnuts	60 mL
¹/₂ cup	chopped red and green cherries	125 mL
¹/₄ cup	chopped raisins	60 mL

1. Combine flour, baking powder, salt, brown sugar and spices. Add margarine and mix with electric mixer or pastry blender until crumbly.

2. Combine ²/₃ **OF A CUP** of beer with beaten egg. Blend with flour mixture. Fold in walnuts, cherries and raisins. Spread batter into an 8″ (20 cm) greased microwave ring mold.

3. Cover with wax paper and microwave on MEDIUM LOW 10 to 11 minutes. Cool 10 minutes before removing from pan.

Drizzle with Cinnamon or Orange Glaze. See page 17.

*Use remaining beer with discretion!!

Chopped raisins give more flavor than whole raisins.

Bars, Slices and Squares

Chewy Bars

These bars taste much like the Crispy Crunch Chocolate bars.

Bottom Crust

¹/₂ cup	**butter or margarine, soft**	125 mL
¹/₂ cup	**brown sugar**	125 mL
¹/₄ cup	**corn syrup**	60 mL
2 cups	**oatmeal**	500 mL

Topping

¹/₂ cup	**chocolate chips**	125 mL
¹/₃ cup	**chunky peanut butter**	75 mL

1. For bottom crust, beat together butter, brown sugar and corn syrup. Add oatmeal and mix well. Press into the bottom of an 8" (20 cm) pie plate.

2. Microwave uncovered, for 2¹/₂–3¹/₂ minutes on MEDIUM. Set aside.

3. Place chocolate chips and peanut butter in a 1 cup measure. Microwave on MEDIUM HIGH 1–1¹/₂ minutes or until the chocolate has melted. Stir until smooth.

4. Spread chocolate/peanut butter mixture over top of the crust. Cut into squares BEFORE refrigerating.

Nanaimo Bars

What can you say about Nanaimo Bars! Everybody's Favorite!

Bottom Layer

½ cup	butter or margarine	125 mL
¼ cup	brown sugar	60 mL
1	egg	1
¼ cup	unsweetened cocoa	60 mL
2 cups	crushed graham wafer crumbs	500 mL
1 cup	coconut, flaked	250 mL
½ cup	chopped walnuts or pecans	125 mL

Filling

¼ cup	butter or margarine, softened	60 mL
¼ cup	milk	60 mL
2 tbsp.	Birds Custard powder OR Vanilla Pudding Mix	30 mL
1½ cups	powdered sugar	375 mL

Topping

¾ cup	chocolate chips	175 mL
2 tbsp.	butter or margarine	30 mL
1 tbsp.	milk	15 mL

1. In a mixing bowl, melt butter. Add sugar and whisk in egg and cocoa. Microwave 2–3 minutes uncovered, on MEDIUM HIGH until slightly thickened, resembling custard. Add crumbs, coconut and walnuts. Press evenly into the bottom of an 8" × 8" (20 cm) square pan. Refrigerate while making the filling.

2. For filling, cream together butter, milk, custard powder and powdered sugar. Spread filling over the bottom crust.

3. For topping, place chocolate chips in a 2 cup measure, add butter and milk. Microwave uncovered, on MEDIUM HIGH 1–2 minutes. Stir until smooth, and pour over filling. Chill and cut into squares.

Microtip
If you choose to make a square in a round pan, try cutting into diamond shapes. They look pretty!

Variation
Kahlua Nanaimo Bars
Add 2 tbsp. Kahula or your favorite liqueur to the filling.

Creme de Menthe Nanaimo Bar
Replace topping in Nanaimo Bar recipe with Creme de Menthe Frosting, page   .

Coconut Topped Raisin Bars

¹⁄₃ cup	butter	75 mL
1 cup	brown sugar	250 mL
1	egg, beaten	1
¹⁄₂ tsp.	vanilla	2 mL
²⁄₃ cup	flour	150 mL
¹⁄₂ tsp.	baking powder	2 mL
¹⁄₄ tsp.	salt	1 mL
¹⁄₂ cup	chopped raisins	125 mL
¹⁄₃ cup	shredded coconut, toasted	75 mL

1. In a microwave mixing bowl, melt butter on HIGH 1 minute. Blend in sugar, add beaten egg and vanilla.

2. Combine flour, baking powder and salt together. Stir into egg and butter mixture and add raisins.

3. Spread in an 8″ × 8″ pan and sprinkle coconut on top.

4. Microwave 5 to 6 minutes on MEDIUM HIGH, then 1 to 2 minutes on HIGH. Let stand a few minutes before cutting into bars.

Yields 16 — 2″ bars.

See photo, page 46.

Chocolate Apricot Bars

Crust

³/₄ cup	flour	175 mL
3 tbsp.	sugar	45 mL
¼ cup	margarine	60 mL
½ cup	apricot jam	125 mL

Chocolate Filling

⅓ cup	flour	75 mL
¼ cup	cocoa	60 mL
¼ tsp.	baking powder	1 mL
⅛ tsp.	salt	pinch
½ cup	margarine, melted	125 mL
3 tbsp.	sugar	45 mL
2	eggs, beaten	2
1 tsp.	vanilla	5 mL

Crisp Topping

½ cup	flour	125 mL
2 tbsp.	white sugar	30 mL
1 tbsp.	brown sugar	15 mL
⅓ cup	margarine	75 mL
⅓ cup	walnuts	75 mL

1. For crust, combine flour and sugar mixing well. Cut in margarine with electric mixer until crumbly. Lightly press mixture into a 9" pie or quiche pan. Microwave on MEDIUM HIGH 2–3 minutes or until crust is dry. Spread apricot jam over cooked crust. Set aside.

2. For filling, combine flour, cocoa, baking powder and salt.

3. In a separate measure combine melted margarine, sugar, beaten eggs and vanilla. Beat until smooth.

4. Combine dry with liquid ingredients. Microwave on MEDIUM 1–1½ minutes or until chocolate mixture just begins to thicken. Stir.

5. Spread cooked chocolate filling on top of apricot layer. Refrigerate until completely cooled.

6. For topping, combine flour and sugars and mix well. Cut in butter until crumbly. Fold in walnuts. Microwave on HIGH 4–5 minutes or until crumbs begin to turn a golden brown. Set aside to cool. The crumbs will become very crunchy after cooling down.

7. Sprinkle cooled crumbs evenly over chocolate filling. Bring to room temperature before serving.

Gambier Bars

This recipe was given to us by The Oven Door Bakery on Bowen Island, B.C. The filling and topping are similar to Nanaimo Bars, with a crunchy peanut butter base.

Bottom Crust

½ cup	brown sugar	125 mL
½ cup	corn syrup	125 mL
1 cup	peanut butter	250 mL
1 cup	rice crispies	250 mL
2 cups	corn flakes	500 mL

1. In a glass mixing bowl, combine brown sugar and corn syrup. Microwave uncovered on HIGH 2 to 3 minutes or until sugar is melted. Add peanut butter to syrup and blend until smooth.

2. Fold in rice crispies and cornflakes. Press into the bottom of a 9″ × 9″ (23 cm) pan.

Filling

¼ cup	butter, softened	60 mL
¼ cup	milk	60 mL
2 tbsp.	vanilla custard powder	30 mL
2 cups	icing sugar	500 mL

1. Combine filling ingredients and mix until smooth. Spread evenly over bottom crust.

Topping

¾ cup	chocolate chips	175 mL
2 tbsp.	butter	30 mL
1 tbsp.	milk	15 mL

1. In a one cup measure, combine chocolate chips, butter and milk. Microwave uncovered, on HIGH 1 to 1½ minutes. Stir until smooth.

2. Spread evenly over filling. Cool and cut into squares. Refrigerate. This freezes well.

Yields 16 — 2″ squares.

See photo, page 46.

Chocolate Oatmeal Brownies

³/₄ cup	semi sweet chocolate chips	175 mL
¹/₂ cup	margarine	125 mL
¹/₂ cup	brown sugar, firmly packed	125 mL
1 tsp.	vanilla	5 mL
2	eggs, beaten	2
³/₄ cup	quick cooking oats	175 mL
¹/₂ cup	flour	125 mL
¹/₂ tsp.	baking powder	2 mL

1. Place chocolate chips and butter in a large bowl. Microwave uncovered, on HIGH 1–2 minutes or until melted. Stir until smooth.

2. Add brown sugar, vanilla and beaten eggs. Stir until well combined. Blend in oats, flour and baking powder to egg mixture. Combine till smooth.

3. Pour batter into a 9" (23 cm) quiche or pie pan. Cover and microwave on MEDIUM 6–7 minutes or until center is cooked. Cool and frost with Cocoa Butter Cream.

Cocoa Butter Cream Frosting

¹/₃ cup	cocoa	75 mL
1¹/₂ cups	powdered sugar, divided	375 mL
¹/₃ cup	margarine, soft	75 mL
1 tbsp.	corn syrup	15 mL
2 tbsp.	milk	30 mL
1 tsp.	vanilla	5 mL

1. In a mixing bowl, blend cocoa and ¹/₂ cup powdered sugar with the margarine. Mix in corn syrup.

2. Add remaining sugar, milk and vanilla. Beat until smooth. Spread over Brownies.

Yields 1 cup.

Variations
1. Add 1 tsp. powdered instant coffee OR 1 tsp. cinnamon.
2. Add 1¹/₂ tsp. grated orange peel and 2 tbsp. orange juice in place of milk.
3. Add 1 tsp. almond OR peppermint flavoring in place of vanilla flavoring.

Butterscotch Brownies

¹/₂ cup	margarine	125 mL
1¹/₄ cups	brown sugar	310 mL
2	eggs, slightly beaten	2
1 tsp.	butterscotch or vanilla flavoring	5 mL
1 cup	flour	250 mL
¹/₂ tsp.	salt	2 mL
1 cup	coconut	250 mL
¹/₂ cup	chopped pecans or walnuts	125 mL

1. In a mixing bowl, melt margarine on HIGH 1 minute. Add brown sugar, eggs and flavoring. Stir until smooth. Add flour, salt, coconut and pecans.

2. Place in a round 9″ (23 cm) pan and microwave covered, on HIGH for 3 to 4 minutes. Cool.

Brownies may be iced if desired. Melt ¹/₂ cup chocolate chips with 1 tsp. butter and spread evenly over brownies or frost with Caramel Icing, page

See photo, page 46.

Chocolate Brownies

Brownies as we know them should be moist and slightly chewy. These are great!

¹/₂ cup	melted margarine	125 mL
1¹/₄ cups	brown sugar	310 mL
2	eggs	2
2 tsp.	vanilla	10 mL
¹/₄ cup	milk	60 mL
3 tbsp.	unsweetened cocoa	45 mL
1¹/₄ cups	flour	310 mL
¹/₂ cup	chopped walnuts	125 mL

1. Stir melted margarine and brown sugar until smooth. Beat in eggs, vanilla and milk.

2. Combine cocoa and flour. Add to creamed mixture and fold in walnuts. Spread batter into an 8″ (20 cm) microwave pan.

3. Microwave covered, on MEDIUM HIGH 5 to 6 minutes. Frost with Creme de Menthe Page 161, or Creole Frosting Page 115.

Butterscotch Raisin Slice

¼ cup	margarine	60 mL
¾ cup	brown sugar	175 mL
1	egg	1
1 tsp.	butterscotch or vanilla flavoring	5 mL
½ cup	flour	125 mL
pinch	salt	pinch
¼ cup	coconut	60 mL
¼ cup	chopped walnuts or pecans	60 mL

1. Soften margarine in a mixing bowl for 20 to 30 seconds on HIGH. Combine with brown sugar and egg, stir till smooth.

2. Add flavoring, flour, salt, coconut and nuts. Mix thoroughly.

3. Spread batter into a 9" (23 cm) pie plate or quiche pan. Microwave on HIGH 2 to 3½ minutes, uncovered, or until completely cooked. Set aside.

Filling

¼ cup	butter	60 mL
½ cup	dark brown sugar	125 mL
2 tbsp.	flour	30 mL
2	eggs	2
¾ cup	dark corn syrup	175 mL
1 tsp.	rum or vanilla extract	5 mL
½ cup	raisins	125 mL

1. Place butter in mixing bowl and microwave on HIGH 20 seconds to soften. Add sugar and flour and beat until smooth. Add remaining ingredients and mix thoroughly.

2. Microwave uncovered, on HIGH 2 to 3 minutes, stirring after every minute. Microwave on MEDIUM an additional 1 or 2 minutes or until mixture has thickened.

3. Pour over crust. Cool completely before slicing.

PIES AND TARTS

Clockwise

Strawberry Pie with Cranberry Glaze
Pumpkin Orange Chiffon Pie
Maid of Honour Tarts
Prune Whips
Rich Lemon Butter Tarts

Crunchy Rhubarb Slice

Precooking gives this topping a tasty, toasted, crunchy appearance.

3 cups	fresh rhubarb*	750 mL
1/4 cup	water	60 mL
3 tbsp.	cornstarch	45 mL
1 1/4 cups	sugar	310 mL
1 tsp.	vanilla	5 mL
3 oz. pkg.	strawberry jello	85 g

Crust

1 cup	flour	250 mL
1/2 cup	coconut	125 mL
1 1/2 cups	quick cooking oatmeal	375 mL
1 cup	brown sugar	250 mL
3/4 cup	margarine	175 mL
1/2 cup	chopped nuts	125 mL

1. Place rhubarb, water, cornstarch and sugar in a large bowl. Microwave on HIGH, uncovered, for 10 minutes or until thickened. Add vanilla and jello. Set aside.

2. For crust, combine flour, coconut, oatmeal and sugar. Cut in butter and mix until crumbly. Stir in nuts.

3. Pat 3 cups of crumb mixture into the bottom of a 10" (25 cm) pie pan. Microwave crust, uncovered on MEDIUM 4 to 5 minutes.

4. Put remaining crumbs in a large glass bowl and microwave on HIGH, uncovered 4–6 minutes, stirring after each minute. Mixture will become crunchy. Set aside to cool.

5. Pour cooled rhubarb over cooked crust and sprinkle with crumbs. Dessert must be chilled in order to cut into slices or squares.

Variation
Lemon Blueberry Crunch
Use blueberries and lemon Jell-o in place of the rhubarb and strawberry jello.

*If using frozen rhubarb, eliminate 1/4 cup of water.

Arabian Date Slice

A date lover's delight!

Base

½ cup	butter or margarine	125 mL
⅓ cup	brown sugar	75 mL
1 tsp.	vanilla	5 mL
1 cup	flour	250 mL
1 tsp.	baking powder	5 mL

1. Combine above ingredients in large bowl and mix with electric mixer or pastry blender until crumbly.

2. Pat firmly into a round 9″ (23 cm) cake or quich pan. Microwave uncovered, on HIGH 2½ to 3 minutes.

Topping

1 cup	dates	250 mL
½ cup	water	125 mL
½ cup	brown sugar	125 mL
2 tsp.	grated orange rind	10 mL
2	egg whites, stiffly beaten	2

1. Combine dates and water. Microwave uncovered, on HIGH 2½ to 3 minutes until soft. Stir until thoroughly combined. Add brown sugar and grated orange rind.

2. Fold in beaten egg whites. Spoon evenly over cooked base. Microwave covered, on HIGH 2½ to 3 minutes. Cool and slice.

Yields about 16 squares.

When a recipe calls for chopped dates, soften a few seconds in the microwave first. It makes chopping much easier.

Dream Squares

This can be made in 10 minutes or less!

24	Graham Wafer Crackers	24
1 cup	brown sugar	250 mL
½ cup	butter	125 mL
½ cup	milk	125 mL
1 cup	graham wafer crumbs	250 mL
1 cup	chopped walnuts	250 mL
1 cup	flaked coconut	250 mL
¼ cup	chopped glaced cherries	60 mL

1. In a 9″ (23 cm) square cake pan, place a layer of graham wafers, cutting to fit the bottom (approximately 12 wafers).

2. Combine brown sugar, butter and milk in a mixing bowl and microwave HIGH 4 to 5 minutes or until boiling.

3. Immediately add the crumbs, walnuts, coconut and cherries. Mix together thoroughly. Spread over graham crackers.

4. Top with remaining crackers, trimming to fit the dish. Press down evenly. Let cool. Ice with Butter Icing.

Butter Icing

¼ cup	butter, softened	60 mL
1 cup	powdered sugar	250 mL
1 tsp.	vanilla or almond flavoring	5 mL

1. Mix together the above ingredients until smooth adding a few drops water or milk for an easy spreading consistency.

See photo, page 45.

As chocolate chips contain some paraffin they do not lose their shape when melted in the microwave. Do not overcook and stir frequently.

Pies, Tarts and Cheesecakes

Pastry

Although a single pastry shell can be microwaved successfully, we feel it is best done in the conventional oven. A pastry shell takes only a few minutes longer in the oven and has that traditional 'brown' appearance. When using a frozen pastry shell, microwave it on HIGH one or two minutes just to get it started and then put in the conventional oven.

A few basic rules to follow for good pastry are: —

1. Have all ingredients as cold as possible
2. Handle mixture lightly, overhandling produces tough pastry
3. Chill rich pastries before baking to prevent 'shrinking'
4. For a plain pastry, use ⅓ as much shortening as flour
5. For a richer, dessert pastry, use ½ as much shortening as flour

Never Fail Pastry

2 cups	flour	500 mL
½ tsp.	salt	2 mL
½ tsp.	baking powder	2 mL
2 tsp.	brown sugar	10 mL
1 cup	shortening	250 mL
1	egg, slightly beaten	1
2 tbsp.	cold water	30 mL
1 tbsp.	lemon juice	15 mL

1. Mix flour, salt, baking powder and brown sugar together. Cut in shortening with a pastry blender until crumbly.

2. Mix egg, water and lemon juice together. Add to flour a little at a time, using enough to bind mixture, form into a ball. Refrigerate a few minutes to cool.

Yields about 1¼ lbs. Enough dough for 2 pie shells or 1 pie shell and 12 tarts.

Strawberry Pie with Cranberry Glaze

Bright and beautiful, a summer treat when strawberries are plentiful. This should be started early in the day, or the night before serving.

1 – 8"	cooked pastry shell	20 cm
4 cups	fresh strawberries	1 L
1 cup	sugar	250 mL
	orange juice or water	
1/3 cup	cornstarch	75 mL
1 cup	cranberries	250 mL
	whipped cream or fresh whole strawberries for garnish	

1. Wash and hull strawberries. Add sugar and let stand, covered about 4 hours to extract juice.

2. Drain strawberry juice into a 4 cup measure and add enough orange juice or water to make 1³/₄ cups liquid.

3. In a custard cup blend cornstarch with a little strawberry juice, return to the measuring cup and mix thoroughly.

4. Microwave on HIGH 2 minutes, add cranberries and microwave HIGH 2 to 3 minutes until thickened and clear. Let cool slightly.

5. Stir strawberries into cranberry glaze and pour into baked pie shell. Refrigerate until set. Decorate with fresh sliced strawberries or whipped cream.

See photo on page 64.

To extract juice from lemons, limes, oranges or grapefruit, place in the microwave for 15 to 20 seconds before cutting or zesting.

Lemon Meringue Pie

1 – 9"	precooked pastry shell or graham wafer crumb crust see page	23 cm
⅓ cup	cornstarch	75 mL
1½ cup	sugar	375 mL
¼ tsp.	salt	1 mL
1½ cups	cold water	375 mL
3	egg yolks, beaten	3
3 tbsp.	butter	45 mL
⅓ cup	lemon juice	75 mL
2 tbsp.	lemon rind	30 mL
3	egg whites	3
2 tbsp.	powdered sugar	30 mL

1. Mix cornstarch, sugar and salt in an 8 cup measure, whisk in cold water. Microwave, uncovered, on HIGH 4–5 minutes or until thickened.

2. Add a little of the hot mixture to the beaten egg yolks. Return egg yolk to the hot mixture and whisk until combined.

3. Add lemon juice and rind to hot mixture and microwave, uncovered, on HIGH an additional 1½–2 minutes.

4. Pour thickened lemon into cooked pie shell.

5. Beat egg whites with powdered sugar and spread over top of pie.

6. Microwave 1–1½ minutes or until meringue is set. Sprinkle with 2 tbsp. of graham wafer crumbs or place pie in a preheated 350 degree oven for 8–10 minutes until meringue is golden.

Tangy Orange Meringue Pie

A refreshing change from Lemon Meringue Pie, oranges are always in season.

1 – 9"	prebaked pastry shell	23 cm
³/₄ cup	sugar	175 mL
¹/₄ cup	cornstarch	60 mL
¹/₄ tsp.	salt	1 mL
1 tsp.	grated orange peel	5 mL
¹/₂ cup	orange juice concentrate	125 mL
1¹/₂ cups	freshly squeezed orange juice	375 mL
3	eggs, separated	3
2 tbsp.	margarine	30 mL
1 tsp.	vanilla	5 mL
2 tbsp.	powdered sugar	30 mL

1. In a large bowl, combine sugar, cornstarch, salt and orange peel. Whisk in orange concentrate and orange juice. Microwave uncovered, on HIGH 3–4 minutes or until thickened, stirring once or twice.

2. Beat egg yolks and combine with ¹/₂ cup of the hot mixture. Return egg yolks to remaining hot mixture. Microwave on HIGH, an additional 2 minutes.

3. Pour filling into cooked pastry shell. Beat egg whites until foamy. Add powdered sugar and beat until stiff peaks form. Spoon meringue over pie. Microwave ¹/₂ to 1 minute on HIGH. The meringue will stay white. Pop under the broiler for a few seconds to brown if desired. If you prefer a more conventional meringue, bake in a preheated oven at 350 degrees for 8–10 minutes or until meringue is golden.

Variation
Orange Chiffon Pie
Fold beaten egg whites into cooled orange filling. Garnish with whipped cream, if desired, and Sugared Orange Peel, see page 159.

Fresh Lime Coconut Pie

This is a refreshing taste treat, similar to Lemon Meringue Pie. The recipe originated in St. Lucia. TRY IT, YOU'LL LIKE IT!

1 – 9″	baked and cooled pastry shell	23 cm
1 cup	sugar	250 mL
¹/₂ cup	cornstarch	125 mL
1¹/₂ cups	hot water	375 mL
3	eggs, separated	3
3 tbsp.	butter	45 mL
2 tsp.	grated lime rind	10 mL
¹/₃ cup	fresh lime juice	75 mL
¹/₂ cup	shredded coconut	125 mL
1 tsp.	vanilla	5 mL
2 tbsp.	sugar	30 mL

1. In a 4 cup (1 L) mixing bowl, combine sugar and cornstarch. Mix thoroughly. Blend in water. Microwave on HIGH, uncovered, 3 to 4 minutes, stirring every minute.

2. Beat egg yolks and gradually stir in a little of the hot sugar mixture. Pour yolk mixture into remaining sugar mixture and blend thoroughly. Microwave on MEDIUM HIGH, uncovered, 2 to 3 minutes until thickened.

3. Add butter, lime rind, juice, coconut and vanilla to cooked sugar mixture. Stir thoroughly to blend. Pour into prepared pie crust and cool completely.

4. Beat egg whites until frothy. Gradually beat in 2 tbsp. sugar and beat until stiff peaks form. Pile on top of pie and microwave on HIGH, uncovered, for 30 seconds.

Microtip
The meringue will not brown in the microwave. To give it color, top with a little toasted coconut or pop under the broiler for a few seconds.

Helpful Hint
Egg whites have only 15 calories each, so if you are on a diet eat the meringue and give away the pie!

Coconut Cream Pie

1 – 9"	cooked pastry shell*	23 cm
³/₄ cup	sugar	175 mL
¹/₄ cup	cornstarch	60 mL
¹/₄ tsp.	salt	1 mL
3 cups	milk	750 mL
1¹/₃ cups	flaked coconut	300 mL
3	eggs, beaten	3

1. Combine sugar, cornstarch and salt in a 2 quart (2 L) bowl. Stir well and whisk in milk and coconut. Microwave uncovered 6 to 7 minutes or until mixture begins to thicken.

2. Stir 2 tbsp. of hot mixture into beaten egg yolks. Whisk egg yolk mixture back into cream mixture. Microwave uncovered on HIGH 1¹/₂ to 2 minutes. Whisk until smooth and pour cream mixture into cooked pie shell. Cool completely and refrigerate.

*See our pastry recipe on page 68.

Toast ¹/₂ cup coconut with 1 tsp. butter in a 2 cup measure in HIGH 1–1¹/₂ minutes, or until coconut just begins to turn a golden brown. Stir every 30 seconds. Watch carefully as coconut browns quickly.

Banana Cream Pie

Cream fillings in the microwave are easy to cook with no threat of scorching. Cooking the bananas with the filling enhances the flavour.

1 – 9"	cooked pastry shell*	23 cm
³/₄ cup	sugar	175 mL
¹/₄ cup	cornstarch	60 mL
¹/₄ tsp.	salt	1 mL
3 cups	milk	750 mL
1 tsp.	vanilla	5 mL
3	egg yolks, beaten	3
3	ripe bananas	3
3	egg whites	3
2 tbsp.	powdered sugar	30 mL
1 tsp.	vanilla	5 mL

1. Combine sugar, cornstarch and salt in a 2 quart (2 L) bowl. Stir well and whisk in milk and vanilla. Microwave uncovered, 5 to 6 minutes or until mixture begins to thicken.

2. Stir 2 tbsp. of hot mixture into the beaten egg yolks. Whisk egg yolk mixture back into cream mixture. Slice 3 bananas into partially thickened cream mixture. Microwave uncovered on HIGH 1¹/₂ to 2 minutes. Pour banana cream mixture into cooked pie shell.

3. Beat egg whites with powdered sugar until stiff peaks form, add vanilla. Spread over cream filling and bake in a 350 degree oven for 10 minutes until golden brown. Cool completely and refrigerate.

*Try our pastry shell on page 68. You just might like it.

Variation
For a change from meringue, whip 1 cup whipping cream with 2 tbsp. powdered sugar until firm. Fold the beaten egg whites into the thickened filling and spoon the whipped cream over top.

Pecan Streusel Pie

Apple pie at its best. A nice change with a crunchy pecan streusel topping. Combination cooking in this recipe brings out the full flavour and texture of the apples.

1 – 9"	uncooked pastry shell	23 cm
Filling		
³/₄ cup	sugar	175 mL
3 tbsp.	flour	45 mL
1 tbsp.	cinnamon	15 mL
¹/₄ tsp.	nutmeg	1 mL
¹/₄ tsp.	salt	1 mL
2 tbsp.	chilled butter	30 mL
8	large apples, peeled, cored and sliced	8
Streusel Topping		
¹/₃ cup	flour	75 mL
¹/₂ cup	brown sugar	125 mL
¹/₄ tsp.	cinnamon	1 mL
¹/₈ tsp.	nutmeg	pinch
¹/₃ cup	chilled butter	75 mL
²/₃ cup	coarsely chopped pecans	175 mL

1. Combine sugar, flour, cinnamon, nutmeg, salt and butter until crumbly. Stir sliced apples into crumb mixture. Place filling in pastry shell.

2. For streusel topping, combine flour, sugar, cinnamon and nutmeg. Cut in butter with pastry blender until mixture is crumbly. Stir in pecans. Sprinkle streusel topping over apples.

3. Preheat conventional oven to 375 degrees. Microwave the pie, uncovered, on HIGH 10–12 minutes. Immediately remove pie from microwave and place in preheated oven for 20 minutes. Serve warm with ice cream or garnish with whip cream.

Pumpkin Orange Chiffon Pie

A light pie perfect to serve after a heavy holiday meal. Even people who don't like pumpkin pie will love this!

1 – 9"	baked pastry pie shell	23 cm
1 tbsp.	unflavored gelatin	15 mL
¼ cup	orange juice	60 mL
3	large eggs, separated	3
1 cup	brown sugar	250 mL
14 oz. can	pumpkin	398 mL
1 tsp.	grated orange rind	5 mL
2 tsp.	cinnamon	10 mL
½ tsp.	ground ginger	2 mL
½ tsp.	salt	2 mL
¼ tsp.	allspice	1 mL
2 tbsp.	sugar	30 mL
1 cup	whipped cream	250 mL
	thin orange slices and pecans for garnish	

1. Sprinkle gelatin over orange juice, microwave 10 to 15 seconds on HIGH to soften.

2. Beat egg yolks in a large microwave mixing bowl. Blend in brown sugar, pumpkin and orange rind. Microwave on HIGH 3 to 4 minutes, or until thickened, stirring with a whisk several times during cooking. Add softened gelatin, cinnamon, ginger, salt and allspice. Stir well and set in refrigerator to cool.

3. When pumpkin mixture is nearly set, beat egg whites with 2 tbsp. sugar until stiff. Fold into pumpkin. Spoon evenly into baked pie shell and chill 3 to 4 hours.

4. Just before serving, decorate with dollops of whipped cream and half slices of orange. Place pecan half on whipped cream.

See photo, page 64.

Microtip
This pie is also very good baked in a ginger crumb crust. (page 85).

Southern Apple Cream Pie

1 – 8″	cooked graham crumb crust or pastry crust	20 cm
3 cups	finely chopped apples (about 3 large apples)	750 mL
1 tsp.	lemon rind	5 mL
½ cup	sugar	125 mL
2 tbsp.	flour	30 mL
1 cup	sour cream or vanilla yogurt	250 mL
2	eggs, beaten	2
1 tsp.	vanilla	5 mL
¼ tsp.	salt	1 mL
	Graham cracker crumbs, chopped walnuts	
	or toasted coconut for topping.	

1. In a small mixing bowl, combine apples and lemon rind. Microwave covered, on HIGH 4 to 5 minutes until apples are tender.

2. In a separate bowl, combine sugar, flour, sour cream, beaten eggs, vanilla and salt.

3. Microwave uncovered, on MEDIUM HIGH 5 minutes, or until slightly thickened, stirring with a whisk after every minute.

4. Combine cooked apples with thickened sour cream mixture. Pour over cooked crust. Sprinkle with topping of your choice and microwave, uncovered on MEDIUM, 1 or 2 minutes.

Make your own chocolate wedges by melting 1 cup chocolate chips and 1 tbsp. butter on MEDIUM HIGH 1 minute. Stir until smooth. Turn a pie plate upside down, cover with a circle of wax paper and spread melted chocolate evenly over circle. Refrigerate until firm. Bring to room temperature before cutting into pie wedges. Place wedges in a decorative fashion in the frosting of that special cake.

Flapper Pie

Never before has flapper pie been so easy and delicious!

Crust

¹/₂ cup	butter, or margarine	125 mL
1¹/₂ cups	graham crackers, finely crushed	375 mL
¹/₄ cup	brown sugar	60 mL
¹/₂ tsp.	cinnamon	2 mL

1. Place butter in a 9″ (23 cm) pie or quiche pan. Microwave on HIGH for 1 minute or until melted. Stir in graham crackers, brown sugar and cinnamon. Press into the bottom and sides of the pie plate, (Reserve 2 tbsp. crumbs for garnish).

2. Microwave uncovered, on HIGH for 1 to 2 minutes. Set aside to cool.

Filling

2 cups	milk	500 mL
¹/₂ cup	powdered sugar	125 mL
¹/₃ cup	cornstarch	75 mL
1 tbsp.	flour	15 mL
3	egg yolks	3
2 tbsp.	butter	30 mL
2 tsp.	vanilla flavoring	10 mL

1. In a large mixing bowl or 4 cup measure, whisk together all of the filling ingredients.

2. Microwave uncovered, on HIGH 5 to 6 minutes or until thickened, whisking 2 or 3 times during cooking.

3. Pour filling into cooked graham crust and spread meringue over top.

Meringue

3	egg whites	3
¹/₂ tsp.	vanilla	2 mL
¹/₄ tsp.	cream of tartar	1 mL
1 tbsp.	sugar	15 mL

1. Beat egg whites until foamy, add vanilla, cream of tartar and sugar and beat until stiff peaks form. Spread meringue over pie and microwave, uncovered on HIGH 1 to 1½ minutes to set the meringue. Sprinkle with reserved crumbs, or brown meringue in a preheated conventional or convection oven for 8–10 minutes at 350 degrees.

Maid Of Honour Tarts

This is another delightful old fashioned recipe that many people will remember. It consists of tart shells, jam and a cake topped with icing. It took time to make and bake them, but it was worth it. Today with pre–cooked tart shells and the microwave, it takes only minutes to prepare and bake.

24	baked tart shells	24
	jam	
½ cup	sugar	125 mL
3 tbsp.	butter	45 mL
1	egg	1
1 tsp.	almond flavoring	5 mL
1 cup	flour	250 mL
⅛ tsp.	salt	pinch
½ tsp.	baking soda	2 mL
½ tsp.	baking powder	2 mL
¼ cup	milk	60 mL

1. In a mixing bowl, combine sugar and butter and beat well. Add egg and beat until light. Add almond flavoring.

2. In a separate bowl, mix together flour, salt, baking soda and baking powder. Add dry ingredients to sugar mixture alternately with milk. Beat until smooth.

3. Place 2 tsp. jam in the bottom of each tart shell. Top each with 1 tbsp. cake batter. Microwave 6 at a time on HIGH 1½ to 2 minutes. Ice with a thin butter icing or Orange Glaze, (page 41). Repeat with remaining shells, jam and batter.

Yields 2 dozen tarts.

See photo, page 64.

Cream cheese will burn easily. Do not overcook.

Dutch Apple Cheesecake

An interesting variation of cheesecake, utilizing apples as a filling. It is really delicious and simple to make.

¹/₄ cup	butter	60 mL
1¹/₄ cups	graham cracker crumbs	310 mL
¹/₂ tsp.	cinnamon	2 mL
2 tbsp.	powdered sugar	30 mL
2	apples	2
2 tbsp.	sugar	30 mL
1 tsp.	cinnamon	5 mL
1 tsp.	flour	5 mL
1–2 tbsp.	water	15–30 mL
12 oz.	cream cheese	375 g
¹/₂ cup	sugar	125 mL
2	eggs	2
2 tbsp.	lemon juice	30 mL
2 tsp.	grated lemon rind	10 mL

1. In a 9" (23 cm) pie plate, microwave butter on HIGH 30 to 40 seconds. Add graham crumbs, cinnamon and powdered sugar. Mix thoroughly. Set aside ¹/₄ cup crumb mixture for topping. Press remaining crumbs evenly over bottom and sides of pie plate. Microwave on HIGH 1 to 1¹/₂ minutes. Set aside.

2. Peel, core and slice apples. In a glass mixing bowl, combine sugar, cinnamon, flour and water. Mix thoroughly with apples.

3. Cover and microwave on HIGH 2 to 3 minutes until apples are tender. Set aside.

4. Soften cream cheese in a 4 cup (1 L) mixing bowl 20 seconds on HIGH. Beat in sugar, eggs, lemon juice and rind.

5. Microwave on HIGH 2 to 3 minutes, whisking every minute. Pour HALF this mixture into cooked pie crust. Microwave 1 or 2 minutes on HIGH, until set.

6. Spread cooked apples over cheesecake and top with remaining cream cheese batter.

7. Microwave 3 to 4 minutes on HIGH or until set in middle. Top with the remaining ¹/₄ cup crumbs. Cool.

Variation
Make a filling using fresh pears in place of the apples.

80

DESSERTS

Clockwise

Watermelon Sorbet
Nancy's Incredibly Easy Orange Mousse
Frozen Chocolate Cream
Bananas Marakesh (apricot filling)

Pineapple Sunburst Cheesecake

A picture pretty pie, nice and light, and not too sweet.

¹/₄ cup	butter	60 mL
1 cup	graham cracker crumbs	250 mL
2 tbsp.	powdered sugar	30 mL
19 oz. can	pineapple tidbits	540 mL
4 oz.	lemon jelly powder	125 g
8 oz.	cream cheese	250 g

1. In a 8" (20 cm) pie pan, microwave butter on HIGH 30 to 40 seconds, or until melted. Combine with graham crumbs and powdered sugar. Press firmly on bottom and sides of pan. Microwave on HIGH 1 to 1¹/₂ minutes. Chill crust while making filling.

2. Drain thoroughly and chill pineapple, reserving juice.

3. In a 4 cup mixing bowl, add enough water to pineapple juice to make 1 cup liquid. Bring to boil on HIGH 2 to 2¹/₂ minutes. Add lemon jelly powder and stir until dissolved.

4. In a separate bowl, soften cream cheese on HIGH 20 seconds. Gradually blend in HALF the gelatin mixture and beat until smooth.

5. Pour into chilled crust. Cool until set.

6. Arrange well drained pineapple tidbits on top of cooled filling in a spiral fashion and spoon remainder of gelatin evenly over all. Cool until gelatin is set. See cover photo.

Microtip
If remaining half of gelatin mixture starts to thicken, heat 10 or 15 seconds to allow it to pour evenly.

Helpful Hint
Fresh pineapple cannot be used as it won't allow the jelly to set.

Aloha Cheesecake

The homemade coconut milk gives this cheesecake a true Polynesian flavor.

Crumb Crust

1¼ cups	graham wafer crumbs	310 mL
2 tbsp.	sugar	30 mL
¼ cup	butter or margarine, melted	60 mL

1. Combine crumbs, sugar and melted butter. Press evenly into the bottom of a 9" (23 cm) pie or quiche pan. Microwave 1 to 1½ minutes on HIGH. Set aside.

Coconut Milk

¾ cup	sweetened coconut	175 mL
¾ cup	milk	175 mL

1. Combine coconut and milk in a 4 cup (1 L) mixing bowl. Microwave uncovered on HIGH 4 to 5 minutes. Strain immediately. Set both aside.

Filling

8 oz pkg.	cream cheese, softened	250 g
2	eggs	2
1 tbsp.	lemon juice	15 mL
¼ cup	powdered sugar	60 mL
1 cup	crushed pineapple	250 mL
	coconut and coconut milk	
	toasted coconut for garnish	

1. In a large mixing bowl, combine cream cheese, eggs and lemon juice. Beat until smooth.

2. Whisk in sugar, pineapple, coconut and coconut milk. Blend thoroughly.

3. Microwave uncovered on HIGH 5 to 6 minutes, stirring after each minute, until mixture has slightly thickened.

4. Pour into cooked pie crust and microwave uncovered on MEDIUM 2 to 3 minutes. Cool completely before serving. Garnish with toasted coconut.

Microtip

To toast coconut, combine 1 tsp. melted butter with 2 tbsp. coconut. Microwave on HIGH 20 to 30 seconds. Watch carefully as this can burn quickly.

Graham Wafer Crumb Crust

1¼ cups	graham wafer crumbs	310 mL
¼ cup	butter	60 mL
2 tbsp.	sugar	30 mL

1. Combine all ingredients in a 4 cup measure and microwave on HIGH 1 minute until butter has melted. Combine thoroughly. Pat onto bottom and sides of an 8″ or 9″ (20 or 23 cm) pie plate. Microwave 1 to 1½ minutes on HIGH. Cool.

Variations

Add 2 to 3 tbsp. (30 to 45 mL) cocoa to crumbs for a Chocolate Crust.

Add ¼ (60 mL) cup finely chopped walnuts.

Add ½ tsp. (2 mL) cinnamon.

Substitute crushed Vanilla Wafers or Ginger Snaps in place of graham wafer crumbs. Omit sugar.

Coconut Crumb Crust

1½ cups	flaked coconut	375 mL
2 tbsp.	butter	30 mL
¼ cup	graham cracker crumbs	60 mL
1 tbsp.	brown sugar	15 mL
1 tsp.	grated orange rind	5 mL

1. Combine all ingredients and microwave on HIGH 1 to 1½ minutes. Stir thoroughly and pat onto bottom and sides of an 8″ or 9″ (20 to 23 cm) pie or quiche pan. Microwave HIGH 30 to 60 seconds.

Crunchy Crumb Crust

¼ cup	butter	60 mL
¼ cup	brown sugar	60 mL
¼ cup	rolled oats	60 mL
¼ cup	flour	60 mL
pinch	salt	pinch
½ cup	corn flakes, slightly crushed	125 mL
¼ cup	finely chopped nuts	60 mL

1. Combine all ingredients thoroughly and pat onto the bottom and sides of a 9″ (23 cm) quiche pan or pie plate. Microwave on HIGH 2 to 3 minutes.

Puddings and Desserts

Raisin Lemon Upside Down Pudding

This easy to assemble pudding is baked over a sweet brown sugar sauce. It is a nice change from cakes and pies. A good dessert at harvest time.

Batter

½ cup	brown sugar	125 mL
1 tbsp.	butter or margarine	15 mL
1 tsp.	baking powder	5 mL
1 cup	flour	250 mL
⅓ cup	chopped raisins	75 mL
1 tsp.	freshly grated lemon rind	5 mL
pinch	salt	pinch
½ cup	milk	125 mL

1. Combine sugar, butter, baking powder and flour. Mix with electric mixer until crumbly.

2. Stir in raisins and lemon rind. Add milk and stir until combined. Cover and set aside.

Sauce

1 cup	brown sugar	250 mL
¼ cup	butter or margarine	60 mL
1 cup	warm tap water	250 mL
pinch	salt	pinch

1. In a 1 quart casserole combine all the sauce ingredients and microwave uncovered, on HIGH 3 to 4 minutes or until rapidly boiling.

2. Spoon batter over sauce. Microwave uncovered, on MEDIUM for 8 to 9 minutes or until the batter is no longer doughy.

3. Serve in dessert bowls and spoon sauce over top.

Serves 4–6.

Apple Dumplings In Lemon Sauce

Dumplings

2	apples, cored, peeled and chopped	2
1/2 cup	sugar	125 mL
1 cup	flour	250 mL
2 tsp.	baking powder	10 mL
1/2 tsp.	salt	2 mL
2 tbsp.	margarine	30 mL
1/2 cup	milk	125 mL
1 tsp.	vanilla	5 mL

Lemon Sauce

1 1/4 cups	hot tap water	310 mL
1 1/2 tsp.	grated lemon rind	7 mL
1/4 cup	lemon juice	60 mL
1/2 cup	sugar	125 mL
2 tbsp.	cornstarch	30 mL
1/4 tsp.	salt	1 mL
2 tbsp.	butter	30 mL

1. In a small bowl, microwave chopped apple on HIGH, covered, 2 to 2 1/2 minutes. Set aside.

2. Combine sugar, flour, baking powder and salt. Cut in margarine and mix with electric mixer or pastry blender until crumbly.

3. Add milk and vanilla, stir until well combined. Batter will be stiff. Cover and set aside.

4. For Lemon Sauce, combine water, lemon rind and juice in a 1 qt. (1 L) casserole. Microwave on HIGH 2 to 3 minutes or until boiling.

5. In a separate bowl, combine sugar, cornstarch and salt. Whisk into boiling lemon water. Microwave on HIGH, uncovered, 4 to 5 minutes or until slightly thickened. Add butter and stir until melted.

6. Drop dumpling batter by large spoonfuls evenly over lemon sauce. Microwave uncovered, on MEDIUM HIGH 7 to 9 minutes. To serve, spoon dumplings into individual dessert dishes and top with lemon sauce. Enjoy!

Serves 6 to 8.

Old Fashioned Washington Pudding

This pudding consists of dumplings cooked over a sweet butterscotch sauce. Easy to prepare with basic ingredients.

1 cup	brown sugar	250 mL
2 tbsp.	butter or margarine, soft	30 mL
2 tbsp.	lemon juice	30 mL
2 cups	water	500 mL
2 tbsp.	cornstarch	30 mL
1/2 cup	sugar	125 mL
1 cup	flour	250 mL
1 tsp.	cinnamon	5 mL
2 tsp.	baking powder	10 mL
2 tbsp.	butter or margarine	30 mL
1/2 cup	milk	125 mL
1/3 cup	chopped raisins, optional	75 mL

1. In a large casserole, whisk brown sugar, butter, lemon juice, water and cornstarch. Microwave uncovered, on HIGH 3–5 minutes or until slightly thickened.

2. While sauce is cooking, combine sugar, flour, cinnamon, and baking powder. Cut in butter until crumbly. Pour in milk, add raisins, and stir until smooth. Batter will be doughy like dumplings.

3. Place large spoonfuls of dumpling batter on top of cooked sauce. Microwave covered, on MEDIUM HIGH for 7–9 minutes or until the dumplings are cooked through.

Serves 6 to 8.

Soften 1/2 cup (125 mL) cold butter 45 seconds on a DEFROST or 30% power.

Apple Cinnamon Bread Pudding

Bread Pudding is remembered by many adults as being a thrifty dessert from their childhood. It was either loved or hated! The current nostalgia for 'down home' foods served in restaurants has brought bread pudding to new heights. On a recent trip to New Orleans, a friend said she had a different bread pudding in restaurants every night for two weeks! Don't limit bread pudding to just bread. Serve with one of the sauces from this book and the combinations are limitless. Remember, it's a good way to use stale breads and buns!

2	large day old cinnamon buns	2
	Butter	
2	apples, peeled, cored and chopped	2
¼ cup	chopped raisins (optional)	60 mL
2 tbsp.	brown sugar	30 mL
pinch	salt	pinch
3	eggs	3
1 cup	cream or milk	250 mL

1. Slice each bun into three layers and butter all cut sides. Cut into cubes.

2. Combine buns, apples, raisins, brown sugar and salt in an 8" cake pan.

3. In a separate mixing bowl, beat eggs and cream thoroughly. Pour over buns. Cover and microwave on HIGH 6 to 7 minutes. Serve plain, with a sauce or whipped cream. Ice cream is a yummy alternative too!

Serves 4.

Pineapple Bread Pudding with Hot Buttery Rum Sauce

¹/₂ cup	margarine	125 mL
²/₃ cup	sugar	150 mL
2	eggs, beaten	2
¹/₂ cup	milk	125 mL
1 tsp.	vanilla	5 mL
14 oz. can	crushed pineapple, drained (reserve juice for sauce)	398 mL
6 cups	bread cubes (8 slices)	1.5 L
1 tbsp.	brown sugar, firmly packed	15 mL
1 tsp.	cinnamon	5 mL

1. In a 2 qt. casserole cream margarine and sugar. Add beaten eggs, milk, vanilla and drained crushed pineapple. Combine until smooth.

2. Stir in bread cubes and smooth pudding out evenly in the casserole. Combine cinnamon and sugar and sprinkle evenly over pudding.

3. Microwave uncovered, on HIGH 7–9 minutes or until completely set.

Hot Buttery Rum Sauce

²/₃ cup	sugar	150 mL
2 tbsp.	cornstarch	30 mL
	add enough water to reserved pineapple juice to make 1 cup	250 mL
¹/₂ cup	butter	125 mL
3 tbsp.	amber rum	45 mL
¹/₃ cup	chopped raisins (optional)	75 mL

1. In a 4 cup measure combine sugar and cornstarch. Whisk in pineapple juice and stir until well combined. Add butter, rum and chopped raisins.

2. Microwave uncovered on HIGH 5–6 minutes or until sauce thickens. Whisk at least once during the cooking time.

This sauce is excellent served over folded dessert crepes, ice cream or cake. Crepe batter page 142.

Genevieve's Carrot Pudding

This was always a favorite traditional Christmas Pudding that normally took 5 to 6 hours to steam on the stove.

2 cups	raisins	500 mL
1 cup	currants	250 mL
2 cups	red and green cherries	500 mL
½ cup	oil	125 mL
1	egg, beaten	1
½ cup	milk	125 mL
1 tbsp.	lemon rind	15 mL
	juice of one lemon	
2 cups	flour	500 mL
1 tsp.	soda	5 mL
2 tsp.	cinnamon	10 mL
1 tsp.	nutmeg	5 mL
1 tsp.	allspice	5 mL
½ tsp.	cloves	2 mL
1½ tsp.	salt	7 mL
⅔ cup	brown sugar	150 mL
2 cups	bread crumbs	500 mL
1 cup	finely shredded carrots	250 mL
1 cup	finely shredded potatoes	250 mL

1. In a 4 cup measure combine raisins and currants. Rinse well, drain, and add just enough water to cover fruit. Microwave uncovered on HIGH for approximately 3–4 minutes or until water just begins to boil and the fruit softens. Drain.

2. In a large mixing bowl, combine drained fruit, cherries, oil, egg, milk, lemon rind and juice. Add remaining ingredients in order given and stir until well combined. Pour batter evenly into a greased 12 cup microwave bundt pan, spread evenly.

3. Microwave uncovered, 20–25 minutes on MEDIUM.

Serve with Lemon Sauce see page 92, or Joy's Christmas Sauce page 162.

Makes 10–12 large servings.

Pear Gingerbread Pudding

An interesting variation of Gingerbread.

Gingercake Batter

¹/₂ cup	brown sugar	125 mL
¹/₄ cup	butter, chilled	60 mL
1¹/₂ cups	flour	375 mL
1 tsp.	baking powder	5 mL
¹/₂ tsp.	baking soda	2 mL
2 tsp.	ginger	10 mL
1 tsp.	cinnamon	5 mL
¹/₂ tsp.	salt	2 mL
¹/₃ cup	molasses	75 mL
¹/₃ cup	hot tap water	75 mL
2	eggs	2

1. Combine sugar, butter, flour, baking powder, baking soda, ginger, cinnamon and salt in a large bowl. Mix with electric beater until mixture resembles cornmeal.

2. In a separate bowl, combine molasses with hot water, whisk in eggs.

3. Add dry ingredients to liquid ingredients and stir until well combined. Cover and set batter aside. Batter will be fairly stiff.

Lemon Sauce

³/₄ cup	sugar	175 mL
1¹/₂ tbsp.	cornstarch	22 mL
¹/₈ tsp.	salt	pinch
1 cup	water	250 mL
3 tbsp.	butter	45 mL
¹/₄ cup	lemon juice	60 mL
¹/₂ tsp.	grated lemon rind	2 mL
2	fresh pears, peeled and sliced	2

1. In a four cup measure, combine sugar, cornstarch and salt. Whisk in water, microwave uncovered, on HIGH 3 to 3¹/₂ minutes or until slightly thickened.

2. Add butter, lemon juice, rind and sliced pears. Microwave an additional 2 minutes on HIGH until pears are tender. Pour into an 8″ (20 cm) cake pan.

3. Spread ginger cake batter over sauce. Microwave uncovered, on MEDIUM HIGH 5 to 6 minutes or until surface no longer appears doughy. Cool for 10 minutes before spooning pudding and sauce into serving dishes.

Serves 6–8.

Tropical Banana Pudding

An excellent pudding served just as is or spooned over Banana Cake, page   .

2¹/₂ cups	milk	625 mL
2 egg	yolks	2
3 tbsp.	flour	45 mL
¹/₂ tsp.	salt	2 mL
¹/₂ cup	powdered sugar	125 mL
2 tbsp.	butter or margarine	30 mL
1 tsp.	banana or vanilla extract	5 mL
¹/₂ cup	crushed pineapple, drained	125 mL
3 medium	bananas — sliced	3
¹/₂ cup	toasted coconut	125 mL
	maraschino cherries to garnish	

1. In a mixing bowl, combine milk with egg yolks, flour, salt and powdered sugar. Whisk until smooth.

2. Microwave uncoverd, on HIGH 3 to 4 minutes or until thickened. Whisk in butter and vanilla.

3. Stir in pineapple and sliced bananas. Pour into 4 dessert bowls. Refrigerate until set. Top each serving with 1 tbsp. toasted coconut and a cherry to garnish.

Yields 4 servings.

Cover scallop shells tightly with aluminum foil, paint the outside of the shell with a thin layer of melted chocolate. Allow to cool and paint a second layer of chocolate over top. Cool thoroughly. Carefully peel the foil from the shell, turn chocolate onto a plate and remove foil carefully. Fill the shell with ice cream and Strawberry Sauce on Page

Chinese Almond Jello

Almond Jello is usually served after Dim Sum, a popular Chinese luncheon. It is light and refreshing and clears the palate.

1 tbsp.	unflavored gelatin	15 mL
2 cups	milk	500 mL
1/3 cup	sugar	75 mL
1 tbsp.	almond extract	15 mL
14 oz. tin	fruit cocktail, undrained	398 mL

1. In a 4 cup measure combine gelatin, milk, and sugar. Microwave uncovered, on HIGH 3 minutes, stirring until sugar has dissolved. Add almond extract and pour jello into a medium size loaf pan. Refrigerate until set.

2. When completely set, cut into cubes and combine with fruit cocktail. Spoon into serving dishes.

Serves 4–6.

Spanish Peaches and Cream

The original name for this dessert is Spanish Cream. The peaches add a nice touch.

1 tbsp.	unflavored gelatin powder	15 mL
1/2 cup	sugar	125 mL
3 cups	milk	750 mL
1 tsp.	vanilla flavoring	5 mL
3	eggs, separated, whites stiffly beaten	3
1 cup	peaches, peeled and chopped	250 mL

1. In a large bowl, combine gelatin, sugar, milk, vanilla and egg yolks. Microwave uncovered on HIGH 2–2½ minutes. Whisk every minute. Fold in stiffly beaten egg whites.

2. Place ¼ cup peaches in the bottom of each of 4 dessert dishes. Pour cream evenly over peaches. (Whisk if cream starts to separate). Garnish with grated nutmeg and a peach slice if desired. Refrigerate 2–3 hours or until firm.

Serves 4.

Rhubarb Torte

In the spring when rhubarb is fresh from the garden, make this treat for the family. Frozen rhubarb may also be used.

Base

³/₄ cup	flour	175 mL
³/₄ cup	rolled oats	175 mL
¹/₂ tsp.	salt	2 mL
¹/₂ tsp.	nutmeg	2 mL
¹/₂ tsp.	cinnamon	2 mL
¹/₄ cup	brown sugar	60 mL
²/₃ cup	melted butter	150 mL

1. Blend all ingredients thoroughly. Press into a 9" (23 cm) round cake or quiche pan. Microwave on HIGH, uncovered, 2 to 2¹/₂ minutes.

Filling

3 cups	rhubarb, cut into ¹/₂" pieces	750 mL
1 tbsp.	cornstarch	15 mL
³/₄ cup	sugar	175 mL
1 tsp.	grated orange rind	5 mL
2	eggs, separated	2
	few drops red food coloring, if desired	
2 tbsp.	sugar	30 mL

1. Place rhubarb in a large mixing bowl. Combine cornstarch and sugar. Mix into rhubarb. Add grated orange rind. Microwave covered, on HIGH 3 to 5 minutes, or until rhubarb is tender.

2. In a separate container, beat egg yolks and slowly add hot juice from rhubarb, mixing well. Microwave on HIGH 2 to 3 minutes, until slightly thickened.

3. Fold cooked rhubarb into egg mixture. Microwave on HIGH 2 minutes. Add red food coloring if desired. Spread mixture on top of crust.

4. For meringue, beat egg whites until frothy. Add 2 tbsp. sugar, beating until stiff peaks form. Pile meringue on top of rhubarb and microwave on HIGH 1 minute.

Shoofly Pie

Many years ago, there was a popular song called "Shoofly Pie and Apple Pan Dowdy". Now we know why it . . . "makes your eyes light up and your tummy say howdy". Shoofly Pie is not a pie at all, but a molasses cake in a pie crust. It is sometimes served hot for breakfast! It is believed the sweetness of the pie attracted flies . . . thus the name "Shoofly."

1 – 9″	cooked pastry shell	23 cm
3/4 cup	water	175 mL
1/2 cup	molasses	125 mL
1/2 tsp.	baking soda	2 mL
1/4 tsp.	ginger	1 mL
1 1/3 cups	flour	225 mL
2/3 cup	brown sugar	150 mL
1 tsp.	cinnamon	5 mL
pinch	salt	pinch
2/3 cup	cold margarine	150 mL

1. Microwave water 2–2 1/2 minutes on HIGH or until boiling. Add molasses, soda and ginger. Stir and set aside.

2. In a mixing bowl, combine flour, sugar, cinnamon and salt. With a pastry blender or electric mixer, cut in cold margarine until crumbly.

3. Alternate layers of 1/3 crumb mixture and half the molasses mixture in the pastry shell, ending with crumb mixture.

4. Microwave on MEDIUM HIGH 6 to 7 minutes or until cake is done and a toothpick inserted in the center comes out clean.

Makes 1 – 9″ pie.

Apple Pan Dowdy

Our version of this old time southern favorite.

Topping

3	apples	3
1 tbsp.	butter	15 mL
¹/₄ tsp.	cinnamon	1 mL
¹/₄ cup	brown sugar	60 mL

Dough

1 cup	flour	250 mL
¹/₄ tsp.	salt	1 mL
1 tsp.	baking soda	5 mL
2 tbsp.	butter	30 mL
¹/₄ cup	brown sugar	60 mL
¹/₄ cup	chopped raisins	60 mL
¹/₂ cup	milk	125 mL

1. Peel, core and slice apples. Add butter, cinnamon and brown sugar. Microwave on HIGH, covered, 2 minutes. Set aside.

2. Combine all dough ingredients and spread evenly in a 9" (23 cm) quiche or cake pan.

3. Spoon cooked apples and juice on top of dough. Microwave uncovered, on HIGH 5 to 6 minutes. Serve warm with cream if desired. Delicious!

Serves 6.

Apple Snow

Apple Snow is a very light, low calorie, dessert. It can be eaten alone, topped with custard, or used as a topping for Gingerbread. Joyce's mom used to make this all the time. Too bad she didn't have a microwave then!

3 to 4	apples	3 to 4
2 tbsp.	sugar	30 mL
1 tbsp.	lemon juice	15 mL
1 tsp.	lemon rind	5 mL
2	egg whites	2

1. Peel, core and chop apples. Combine apples, sugar, lemon juice and rind in a mixing bowl. Microwave covered, on HIGH 3 to 4 minutes until apples are tender.

2. Whip apples with electric mixer or blender to make applesauce.

3. Beat egg whites until stiff. Fold applesauce into egg whites a little at a time. Chill. Serve plain or make a Custard Sauce (page 163) with the left over egg yolks.

Yields 4 servings.

Fruit Tapioca

Tapioca is a light refreshing dessert that can be prepared with ease and speed in the microwave.

2 cups	milk	500 mL
2	eggs, separated	2
1/4 cup	sugar	60 mL
1/4 cup	quick cooking tapioca	60 mL
pinch	salt	pinch
1 tsp.	vanilla or almond flavoring	5 mL
2 cups	fruit, fresh or canned, drained	500 mL

1. In a 4 cup measure, combine milk, egg yolks, sugar, tapioca and salt. Microwave uncovered on HIGH $5^{1}/_{2}$ to $6^{1}/_{2}$ minutes or until tapioca has slightly thickened.

2. Beat egg whites until stiff, add vanilla and fold into thickened tapioca mixture. Add fruit and pour into 6 serving bowls or refrigerate in mixing bowl until ready to serve.

Serves 6.

SLIGHTLY GOURMET

Clockwise from top

Amaretto Trifle
Sherry Pudding in Raspberry Sauce
Nesselrode Pie

Rhubarb Puff

A light as air dessert suitable after a heavy meal. This is similar to Apple Snow.

4 cups	diced, rhubarb	1 L
2 tsp.	unflavoured gelatin	10 mL
¼ cup	cold water	60 mL
½ cup	sugar	125 mL
1 tbsp.	fresh lemon juice	15 mL
2	egg whites	2
2 tbsp.	sugar	30 mL

1. In a mixing bowl, microwave rhubarb, covered, 5 to 6 minutes on HIGH, until tender. You should have about 2 cups hot stewed rhubarb.

2. Add gelatin to cold water, and microwave on HIGH 20 seconds, stir to dissolve.

3. Add dissolved gelatin, sugar, and lemon juice to rhubarb, mixing thoroughly. Let cool. When slightly thickened, whip or blend in food processor until smooth.

4. Beat egg whites with 2 tbsp. sugar until stiff. Fold into rhubarb. Pour into serving dish, or 4 parfait glasses. Let cool until set. Garnish with a dollop of whipped cream and a strawberry on top.

Yields 4 servings.

Helpful Hint
Egg whites beat higher when at room temperature. Warm them in the microwave 5 to 6 seconds, before whipping.

Left over egg yolks may be used to make a custard sauce.

Blueberry Crisp

Keep a package of frozen blueberries on hand for this dessert. Crunchy topping has many uses. Make a double batch and store half.

Crunchy Topping

1 cup	flour	250 mL
1 cup	brown sugar	250 mL
1 tsp.	cinnamon	5 mL
1/2 tsp.	salt	2 mL
1 cup	oatmeal	250 mL
1/2 cup	margarine	125 mL
4 cups	fresh or frozen blueberries	1 L
1/4 cup	powdered sugar	60 mL

1. Combine flour, brown sugar, cinnamon, salt and oatmeal in large glass bowl. Cut in margarine with pastry blender or use electric mixer and mix until crumbly. Microwave, uncovered, on HIGH for 4 to 5 minutes, or until mixture begins to turn a golden brown. Stir after each minute. Set aside. Will become crunchy when cooled.

2. Place blueberries in a 2 quart casserole. Sprinkle with powdered sugar. Place crumb topping over blueberries and microwave uncovered on HIGH for 5 to 8 minutes or until blueberries are heated through. (Fresh berries will take the minimum time.)

Serves 6 to 8.

Variation
Use any sliced fresh fruit of your choice. Use crunchy topping over Deep Dish fruit pies.

Fresh Peach Crisp

Unadorned, or topped with whipped cream or sauce, nothing beats a fresh fruit crisp.

6	fresh peaches	6
2 tbsp.	fresh lemon juice	30 mL
1 tsp.	grated lemon rind	5 mL
1/2 cup	butter	125 mL
3/4 cup	brown sugar	175 mL
1 cup	flour	250 mL
3/4 cup	rolled oats	175 mL
1/4 tsp.	nutmeg	1 mL

1. Peel, pit and slice peaches. Place in a 9" (23 cm) round cake or quiche pan. Sprinkle with lemon juice and grated rind.

2. In a large mixing bowl, soften butter 15 to 20 seconds on HIGH. Blend in brown sugar, add flour, rolled oats, nutmeg and thoroughly combine. Lightly pat crumb mixture on top of the peaches.

3. Microwave on HIGH, uncovered, 6 to 7 minutes or until peaches are cooked and topping is no longer doughy. Serve plain or with NUTMEG SAUCE (Page 18).

Helpful Hint
One average lemon should yield about 1/4 cup juice and 2 tsp. grated rind.

Nancy's Incredibly Easy Orange Mousse

The name says it all, thanks Nancy! Use the best quality orange juice and marshmallows. It does make a difference to the flavor.

12¹/₂ oz. tin	frozen orange juice	355 mL
	grated rind of one orange	
	grated rind and juice of one lemon	
1¹/₄ cups	water	310 mL
50	large marshmallows	50
1 pint	whipping cream	500 mL
	chocolate curls or orange sections for garnish	

1. In a large mixing bowl, combine orange juice, orange rind, lemon rind, lemon juice and water. Microwave on HIGH 4 to 5 minutes until boiling.

2. Add marshmallows, and stir until fully melted. If mixture cools before marshmallows are melted, microwave on LOW a few seconds at a time. Regrigerate until almost jelled. This takes a few hours.

3. Whip cream and fold into the jelly mixture. Pour into 8 individual parfait glasses or an attractive serving bowl. Decorate with chocolate curls or orange sections.

Yields 8 servings.

See photo, page 82.

Make large wide chocolate curls with a vegetable peeler.
To bring 1 square of chocolate to room temperature, microwave 10–20 seconds. Allow to stand 2 minutes.

Cookies

Nut Hermits

These, along with Chocolate Chip cookies were made regularly when Joyce's children were growing up. They took 15 minutes to bake and 3 minutes to eat. Now with the microwave, they still take 3 minutes to eat, but only 2½ minutes to bake!

¼ cup	butter	60 mL
½ cup	sugar	125 mL
1	egg	1
½ cup	flour	125 mL
¼ tsp.	baking powder	1 mL
½ tsp.	cinnamon	2 mL
¼ tsp.	nutmeg	1 mL
¼ tsp.	cloves	1 mL
pinch	salt	pinch
¼ cup	chopped raisins	60 mL
½ cup	chopped walnuts	125 mL

1. In a mixing bowl, beat butter (soften 10 seconds if necessary) and mix in sugar and egg.

2. Combine flour, baking powder, cinnamon, nutmeg, cloves and salt. Stir into butter mixture. Add raisins and walnuts.

3. Grease and flour a piece of wax paper and place it in a flat dish. Drop cookie batter in a circle around the outer edge of the paper. Microwave, uncovered on HIGH 2½ to 3 minutes. Make 8 at a time.

Yields 16 cookies.

Variation
If you wish to make cake–like cookies, add ¼ cup more flour and microwave 8 at a time on MEDIUM HIGH, 3 to 3½ minutes.

Chocolate Chip Oat Cookies

1 cup	quick cooking oats	250 mL
³/₄ cup	flour	175 mL
³/₄ cup	brown sugar	175 mL
¹/₄ tsp.	baking soda	1 mL
¹/₂ tsp.	salt	2 mL
¹/₂ cup	margarine	125 mL
1 tsp.	vanilla	5 mL
¹/₂ cup	chocolate chips	125 mL

1. Combine oats, flour, sugar, soda and salt. Add margarine and vanilla. Blend thoroughly with electric mixer. Add chocolate chips and combine well.

2. Form cookie dough into 1″ balls and place 8 in a circle on a flat dish covered with a piece of lightly floured wax paper. Microwave 2¹/₂ to 3 minutes on HIGH, uncovered. Repeat with remaining dough.

Yields 2 dozen cookies.

Make your own chocolate leaves by melting ¹/₂ cup chocolate chips and 1 tsp. butter about 1 minute on HIGH. Paint the melted chocolate about ¹/₈″ thick onto the washed shiny leaves. (Laurel leaves work well.) Allow to harden in the refrigerator for about 1 hour and peel off when ready to use. See Photo of Nesslerode Pie.

Chocolate Raisin Nut Drops

A quickie cookie/candy. Convenient for snacks or lunch boxes.

1 cup	chocolate chips	250 mL
1 cup	butterscotch chips	250 mL
2 cups	dry chow mein noodles	500 mL
1 cup	peanuts	250 mL
¹/₂ cup	raisins	125 mL

1. In a 2 qt. (2 L) mixing bowl, combine chocolate chips and butterscotch chips. Microwave on HIGH, uncovered, 1 to 2 minutes or until melted. Be careful not to overcook. Stir until smooth.

2. Add noodles, peanuts and raisins. Stir until thoroughly combined. Drop by tablespoonfuls on waxed paper or buttered pan. Cool until firm.

Yields 2 to 2¹/₂ dozen, depending on size.

Oatmeal Fingers

Only four ingredients, nothing could be easier!

²/₃ cup	brown sugar	150 mL
¹/₂ cup	butter	125 mL
2 cups	rolled oats	500 mL
1 tsp.	almond flavoring	5 mL

1. Combine sugar and butter in a 4 cup (1 L) mixing bowl. Microwave on HIGH 2 to 3 minutes, stir until melted and well blended.

2. Add oats and almond flavoring mixing well. Spread on a greased 8″ (20 cm) square pan, ¹/₂″ thick (1.5 cm). Microwave uncovered, 2 to 3 minutes. Cool. Cut into fingers.

Yields about 2 dozen fingers.

See photo, page 46.

Variation
When cooled, dip each end about 1″, into melted chocolate. Let cool on waxed paper.

Butterscotch Oatmeal Cookies

Two dozen cookies can be microwaved in 10 to 12 minutes. The conventional oven takes this much time just to preheat! However, the conventional oven is more suitable when baking large batches of cookies.

1 cup	quick cooking oats	250 mL
³/₄ cup	flour	175 mL
³/₄ cup	brown sugar	175 mL
¹/₄ tsp.	baking soda	1 mL
¹/₂ tsp.	salt	2 mL
¹/₂ cup	butter or margarine	125 mL
1 tsp.	butterscotch flavoring	5 mL
1	egg, beaten	1

1. Combine oats, flour, sugar, baking soda and salt. Add butter and mix with electric mixer until crumbly.

2. Combine flavoring with beaten egg and add to flour mixture. Blend until dough forms a ball.

3. Shape dough into 1" (2.5 cm) round cookies, approximately 1 tbsp. each. Place 8 cookies at a time, in a circle, on a lightly greased shallow dish. Slightly flatten with a fork.

4. Microwave uncovered on MEDIUM for 3 to 3¹/₂ minutes. Repeat with remaining dough.

Yields approximately 2 dozen cookies.

Variations
For the following variations, substitute vanilla for butterscotch flavoring in the above recipe. DO NOT FLATTEN COOKIES.

Thimble Cookies
As soon as the cookies are removed from the microwave, make an imprint with your thumb in the center of each cookie and fill with 1 tsp. jam of your choice. See photo, page 46.

Raisin Oat Cookies
Add ³/₄ cup chopped raisins to the cookie dough.

Spicy Walnut Cookies
Add 1 cup finely chopped walnuts, 1 tsp. nutmeg, 1 tsp. cinnamon and ¹/₄ tsp. allspice to cookie dough.

Wholewheat Date Fingers

Nutritious chewy cookies.

2	eggs	2
½ cup	sugar	125 mL
1 tsp.	grated orange rind	5 mL
½ cup	wholewheat flour	125 mL
1 tsp.	baking powder	5 mL
¼ tsp.	salt	1 mL
1 cup	chopped dates	250 mL
1 cup	chopped walnuts	250 mL
	powdered sugar for coating	

1. In a large mixing bowl, beat eggs until frothy, add sugar and orange rind. Continue beating until creamy.

2. Combine flour, baking powder and salt. Add to egg mixture and beat well. Fold in dates and walnuts.

3. Spread date mixture ½" thick in an 8" (20 cm) microwave pan. Microwave on MEDIUM HIGH, covered, 4 to 5 minutes, until cooked, but still soft. Cut in small squares while still warm and shape into fingers. Roll in powdered sugar.

Yields approximately 2 dozen.

Microtip
Microwave dates 10 or 20 seconds to soften before chopping.

Frozen Desserts

Frozen Chocolate Cream

An appropriate dessert after a heavy meal. Tastes like rich chocolate ice cream. Take out of the refrigerator 10 minutes before serving.

³/₄ cup	sugar	175 mL
1 cup	milk	250 mL
3	eggs, separated	3
¹/₂ tsp.	vanilla	2 mL
¹/₄ cup	chocolate chips, melted	60 mL
1 cup	whipping cream	250 mL

1. Combine sugar, milk and egg yolks in a microwave mixing bowl. Microwave on MEDIUM, uncovered, 5 to 6 minutes or until thickened, stirring every minute.

2. Whisk in vanilla and melted chocolate chips. Refrigerate 10 to 15 minutes.

3. Whip egg whites until stiff. Fold into chocolate mixture.

4. Beat whipping cream and fold into the chocolate mixture.

5. Divide evenly between 6 dessert dishes and freeze until firm. Approximately 1 hour.

Serves 6.

See photo, page 82.

Variations
For **Frozen Chocolate Banana Parfait**, follow above recipe through Step 4. Chill mixture until firm but not frozen. Place layers of chocolate cream, then sliced bananas, into 6 individual parfait glasses, repeating layers, ending with chocolate cream. Freeze.

Add 2 tbsp. Kahlua, Tia Maria or Chocolate Mint Liqueur in place of the vanilla.

Maurgan's Frozen Chocolate Peanut Squares

With the help of the microwave you can whip up a tasty ice cream dessert. Big kids and little kids all love this!

Crust

¼ cup	butter or margarine	60 mL
1½ cups	vanilla or graham wafer crumbs	375 mL
2 tbsp.	sugar	30 mL

Filling

½ cup	butter or margarine, softened	125 mL
1½ cups	powdered sugar	375 mL
3	eggs	3
¾ cup	chocolate chips	175 mL
1 cup	chopped peanuts	250 mL
4 cups	any flavor ice cream, softened	1 L
½ cup	chopped peanuts	125 mL

1. In a bowl, melt butter and stir in crumbs and sugar. Microwave on HIGH 1–2 minutes, stirring frequently. Press cooked crumbs into a 9" × 13" (23 × 33 cm) pan. Freeze for 30 minutes or until firm.

2. In a large bowl, beat butter and powdered sugar until creamy. Beat in eggs, one at a time.

3. Place chocolate chips in a 2 cup measure and microwave on MEDIUM HIGH 1–2 minutes. Stir until melted. Pour melted chocolate into filling.

4. Spread filling over crust and freeze until firm. About 30 minutes.

5. Soften ice cream in a large bowl 30 to 40 seconds on HIGH or JUST long enough to make it spreadable. Spoon softened ice cream over filling and sprinkle with chopped peanuts.

Strawberry Whip

A light frozen dessert so good to serve in the summer, after that barbecued chicken!

2	eggs, separated	2
²/₃ cup	milk	150 mL
²/₃ cup	sugar	150 mL
1 cup	whipping cream	250 mL
1 cup	fresh or frozen strawberries	250 mL
1 tsp.	lemon juice	5 mL

1. In a mixing bowl, combine egg yolks, milk and sugar. Microwave 1 minute on HIGH and then 5 to 6 minutes on MEDIUM, stirring 2 or 3 times. Cool slightly.

2. Beat egg whites until stiff. Whip cream. Fold both into cooled custard mixture.

3. Place strawberries and lemon juice in a blender or food processor and blend until smooth. Stir into custard. Pour into individual serving dishes and freeze until firm.

Serves 4.

Variation
For **Pineapple Whip**, Stir 1 cup crushed, drained pineapple into custard in place of the strawberries.

Frozen Banana Dessert

The taste of fresh banana ice cream. A real treat for banana lovers!

2 tbsp.	lemon jelly powder	30 mL
1/4 cup	water	60 mL
3	bananas, mashed	3
2 tbsp.	lemon juice	30 mL
1/2 cup	sugar	125 mL
1 cup	whipping cream, whipped	250 mL

1. In a small bowl, combine jelly powder and water. Microwave 20 to 30 seconds on HIGH. Stir to dissolve jelly and set aside to cool.

2. Combine mashed bananas, lemon juice (use fresh if possible), and sugar. Microwave on HIGH 2 minutes. Stir and let cool slightly.

3. Add cooled jelly mixture alternately with bananas to the whipped cream. Pour into individual serving dishes, cover and freeze.

Yields 3 cups, approximately 4 servings.

Variation
Instead of freezing in serving dishes, freeze in individual jelly molds, unmold and top with Chocolate Sauce, page 123.

Lemon Ice Cream Pie

1 pint	vanilla ice cream	500 mL
3	eggs, divided	3
½ cup	sugar	125 mL
pinch	salt	pinch
¼ cup	freshly squeezed lemon juice	60 mL
1½ cups	whipping cream, whipped	375 mL

1. Leave ice cream in its container. (Remove any metal.) Microwave on MEDIUM for 1 to 1½ minutes or until just soft enough to spread. Spoon onto bottom and sides of a 9″ (23 cm) quiche pan. Place in freezer until firm, approximately 45 minutes.

2. In a large mixing bowl beat together 1 whole egg and 2 egg yolks, add sugar, salt and lemon juice. Microwave on MEDIUM HIGH, uncovered 1½ to 2 minutes or until thickened. Whisk every 30 seconds. Cool for 10 minutes in the refrigerator.

3. Beat remaining two egg whites until stiff peaks form. Combine the beaten egg whites and the whipped cream. Fold into cooled lemon mixture. Pour all filling into the frozen ice cream shell. Return to freezer.

4. Remove from freezer 10 minutes before serving. Garnish with scored lemon slices or grated lemon rind.

Frostings and Icings

Coconut Frosting

¹/₂ cup	brown sugar	125 mL
1 tsp.	cornstarch	5 mL
1	egg yolk	1
1 small tin	evaporated milk	160 mL
¹/₄ cup	margarine	60 mL
1 tsp.	vanilla	5 mL
¹/₂ cup	coconut	125 mL

1. In a four cup (1 L) measure, combine brown sugar and cornstarch. Beat in remaining ingredients, except coconut.

2. Microwave uncovered, on HIGH, 3 to 4 minutes or until slightly thickened, stirring twice during cooking.

3. Add coconut and mix until combined. Allow to cool before spreading. Use as frosting or filling for a spice or chocolate cake.

Yields approximately 1¹/₂ cups.

Creole Frosting

³/₄ cup	chocolate chips	175 mL
¹/₄ tsp.	cinnamon	1 mL
1 tsp.	instant coffee	5 mL
¹/₄ tsp.	salt	1 mL
¹/₂ cup	sour cream	125 mL

1. In a 2 cup measure microwave chocolate chips on HIGH 1 minute or until melted. Stir in cinnamon, instant coffee and salt until combined.

2. Blend in sour cream. Refrigerate until frosting is thick enough to hold swirls on cake.

Yields enough to frost one 9″ cake.

Honey Seafoam Frosting

These "Seafoam" Frostings are all based on the delicious boiled icing that was so popular, but time consuming years ago. The microwave has changed all that. Try all these combinations and add a few more of your own.

⅓ cup	honey	75 mL
⅓ cup	light corn syrup	75 mL
½ tsp.	baking powder	2 mL
⅛ tsp.	salt	pinch
2	egg whites	2
½ tsp.	vanilla	2 mL

1. In a 2 qt. (2 L) glass mixing bowl with handle, combine honey, corn syrup, baking powder and salt. Microwave uncovered on HIGH 4 to 5 minutes or until syrup reaches the 'hard ball' stage. (This is when syrup forms a hard ball when dropped into cold water).

2. While syrup is cooking, combine egg whites and vanilla in a large bowl and beat until stiff.

3. Slowly pour hot syrup into beaten egg whites, beating continuously until stiff peaks form. Frost top and sides of cooled cake. Recipe may be doubled to fill and frost a layer cake.

Yields enough to frost one 8" cake.

Variations
For **Lemon Honey Seafoam Frosting**, add 1 tbsp. lemon juice and 1 tsp. grated lemon rind in place of the vanilla.

For **Apricot Honey Seafoam Frosting**, add 2 tbsp. of Apricot Honey Butter, in place of the vanilla.

Coffee Seafoam Frosting

1 cup	brown sugar	250 mL
½ tsp.	baking powder	2 mL
⅛ tsp.	salt	pinch
¼ cup	strong coffee	60 mL
2	egg whites	2
1 tsp.	vanilla	5 mL

1. In a 2 qt. (2 L) bowl, combine brown sugar, baking powder and salt. Stir in coffee.

2. Microwave uncovered, on HIGH, 3½ to 4½ minutes until syrup reaches the 'hard ball' stage.

3. In a large bowl, beat egg whites and vanilla until stiff. SLOWLY pour hot syrup into egg whites, beating continuously until stiff peaks form.

Yields enough to frost one 8" cake.

Variation
For **Mocha Seafoam Frosting**, combine 1 tbsp. cocoa with the brown sugar in Step 1. A fantastic frosting for our Chocolate Layer Cake, page 15.

Creamy Orange Icing

This icing will enhance gingerbread, white, chocolate or spice cake.

¼ cup	frozen orange juice concentrate	60 mL
¼ cup	butter or margarine	60 mL
1 cup	powdered sugar	250 mL
1 tbsp.	corn starch	15 mL

1. Combine orange juice concentrate and butter in mixing bowl. Microwave on HIGH uncovered, for 1–1½ minutes or until butter is melted.

2. Combine powdered sugar and cornstarch. Whisk into orange mixture. Microwave 2½–3 minutes or until slightly thickened. Cool.

Garnish with fresh scored orange slices.

Yields approximately 1 cup of icing.

Caramel Icing

³/₄ cup	brown sugar	175 mL
¹/₄ cup	butter	60 mL
¹/₄ cup	milk or cream	60 mL
1 cup	powdered sugar	250 mL
¹/₂ tsp.	vanilla	2 mL

1. In a 1 qt. (1 L) bowl, place brown sugar and butter. Microwave uncovered, on HIGH 2 minutes, or until sugar dissolves. Stir to blend.

2. Add milk or cream. Microwave uncovered, on HIGH an additional 2 to 3 minutes. Add sugar and vanilla, beat until smooth.

Yields approximately 1¹/₂ cups of icing.

Sour Cream Lemon Icing

1 cup	sour cream	250 mL
¹/₂ cup	icing sugar	125 mL
1 tsp.	lemon juice	15ml
3 drops	yellow food coloring, optional	3 drops
	zest of ¹/₂ lemon for garnish	

1. Combine the above until smooth and pour over cooled cake.

2. Sprinkle with lemon zest.

Lemon zest is the extreme outer peel of the lemon.

Sauces, Jams and Syrups

Strawberry Sauce

½ cup	sugar	125 mL
1 tbsp.	cornstarch	15 mL
1 tsp.	grated lemon rind	5 mL
1 tbsp.	lemon juice	15 mL
¼ cup	water	60 mL
2 cups	fresh or frozen strawberries	500 mL

1. In a 4 cup (1 L) mixing bowl, combine sugar, cornstarch and lemon rind. Blend in lemon juice and water. Add strawberries and mix thoroughly. Microwave uncovered, on HIGH for 5–6 minutes or until slightly thickened. If sauce is too thick, add additional water until desired consistency. Excellent served with Sherry Pudding, see Page   .

Yields approximately one cup.

Cranberry Orange Sauce

A beautiful red, tangy sauce. Serve with muffins, cakes, fruit or over ice cream.

1 cup	sugar	250 mL
¼ cup	water	60 mL
¼ cup	orange juice	60 mL
½ tsp.	grated orange rind	2 mL
2 cups	fresh or frozen cranberries	500 mL

1. Combine all ingredients in a large mixing bowl and microwave, covered, on HIGH 2 minutes. Stir.

2. Microwave on HIGH uncovered, an additional 4 to 5 minutes. Stir, cover and refrigerate.

Yields 2 cups.

Hint
This sauce is excellent served with meat and poultry.

Fruit Juice Sauce

Use your imagination and make a fruity sauce to cover left over cake or to serve with ham or ribs.

2 cups	any kind of fruit juice	500 mL
pinch	salt	pinch
1/3 cup	flour	75 mL
1/2 cup	cold water	125 mL
1/3 cup	butter or margarine	75 mL

1. In a 4 cup measure, combine fruit juice and salt.

2. In a 2 cup measure, whisk flour and cold water until smooth. Pour into fruit juice and stir.

3. Microwave uncovered, on HIGH 3–5 minutes or until thickened. Add butter and stir until dissolved.

Tip
Add a handful of chopped fruit or raisins.

Yields approximately 2½ cups.

Honeysuckle Sauce

Lovely served over any fresh fruit or day old cakes.

1 tbsp.	cornstarch	15 mL
2 tbsp.	Southern Comfort	30 mL
1 tbsp.	lemon juice	15 mL
1/2 cup	orange juice	125 mL
1/2 cup	powdered sugar	125 mL
1/4 cup	honey	60 mL
2	eggs, well beaten	2
1 cup	cream, whipped	250 mL

1. In a large mixing bowl, combine cornstarch and Southern Comfort.

2. Whisk in juices, sugar, honey and eggs. Microwave, uncovered on HIGH 2–3 minutes or until thickened.

3. Cool completely and fold in whipped cream.

Yields approximately 2 cups of sauce.

Almond Strawberry Sauce

Spoon over cake or pudding for a quick, elegant dessert. Substitute any fresh fruit for the strawberries.

2 tbsp.	butter	30 mL
1 tbsp.	sugar	15 mL
1/2 cup	sliced almonds	125 mL
3 cups	fresh hulled strawberries, sliced	750 mL
1/4 cup	sugar	60 mL
2 tbsp.	cornstarch	30 mL
1/2 tsp.	almond flavoring	2 mL

1. In a large bowl, combine butter and sugar. Microwave uncovered, on HIGH for 1 minute or until butter has completely melted.

2. Stir in almonds and microwave an additional 2 to 3 minutes or until almonds just begin to turn golden. Stir twice each minute.

3. Add strawberries, sugar, cornstarch and almond flavoring to toasted almonds. Microwave 3–4 minutes or until slightly thick-ened. If sauce thickens too much after being chilled, add 2 tbsp. of water.

Yields approximately 2 cups.

Marshmallow Sauce

1 cup	sugar	250 mL
1/2 cup	water	125 mL
16	large marshmallows	16
2	egg whites, stiffly beaten	2
1/2 tsp.	vanilla flavoring	2 mL

1. In a large bowl, combine sugar and water. Microwave uncovered, on HIGH 3–4 minutes until syrupy. Fold in marshmallows and stir until melted. Microwave an additional 30 seconds if necessary.

2. Fold in beaten egg whites and add flavoring. Excellent for home-made sundaes.

Yields approximately 1 1/2 cups.

Fresh Fruit Dressing

This is delicious poured over any combination of fresh fruit or it can be used as a fruit dip.

1 lemon	juice and rind	1
2 oranges	juice and rind	2
1 cup	sugar	250 mL
1 egg	well beaten	1

1. Strain fruit juices into a two cup measure. Add sugar and beaten egg. Whisk until smooth.

2. Microwave uncovered, on HIGH 2–3 minutes or until thickened. Cool and serve.

Yields ³/₄–1 cup dressing.

Apricot Honey Butter

A deluxe spread for toast, fruit bread, muffins, and cakes. Excellent added to butter cream frostings for a sumptuous variation.

3 cups	fresh apricots (approx. 1¹/₂ lbs.)	750 mL
¹/₄ cup	water	60 mL
³/₄ cup	sugar	175 mL
¹/₄ cup	honey	60 mL
2 tsp.	grated orange rind	10 mL

1. Cut, pit and halve apricots into a 2 qt. (2 L) bowl. Add water, cover and microwave on HIGH for 5 minutes or until fruit has softened.

2. Puree fruit in blender or food processor until smooth. Add sugar, honey and orange rind to pureed fruit.

3. Cover and microwave on HIGH for 3 minutes or until mixture begins to boil. Remove cover, microwave on MEDIUM HIGH for an additional 12 to 14 minutes or until slightly thickened. Stir once or twice during cooking. Refrigerate.

Yields 1¹/₂ cups.

Variation:
Apple Honey Butter
Use apples in place of apricots, following the above steps, substituting lemon rind for orange rind.

Peach Honey Butter
Use peaches in place of apricots, following the above steps.

Chocolate Sauce

Good topping for ice cream as it won't harden. Keep in refrigerator. (You might have to hide it!)

1 cup	brown sugar	250 mL
¼ cup	cocoa	60 mL
2 tbsp.	corn syrup	30 mL
⅓ cup	hot tap water	75 mL
½ tsp.	vanilla	2 mL
1 tbsp.	butter	15 mL

1. In a 4 cup measure, combine sugar and cocoa. Blend in corn syrup, water, vanilla and butter. Mix until smooth.

2. Microwave uncovered, on HIGH 3 to 4 minutes, whisking every minute.

Yields 1 cup.

Butterscotch Sauce

A sauce for butterscotch connoisseurs

2	egg yolks	2
½ cup	butter, melted	125 mL
½ cup	water	125 mL
1 cup	brown sugar	250 mL

1. Combine all of the above ingredients in a 4 cup measure and stir until smooth. Microwave uncovered, on HIGH 3–5 minutes or until thickened. Cool and serve over ice cream or any cake.

Yields approximately 1½ cups.

Super Easy Rhubarb Jam

Let your imagination run wild with this. Try different fruits and gelatins. Prepare rhubarb the night before.

4 cups	chopped rhubarb	1 L
3 cups	sugar	750 mL
2 tsp.	grated orange rind	10 mL
1 pkg.	strawberry jelly powder	85 g

1. Combine rhubarb and sugar. Leave overnight, covered.

2. Microwave rhubarb and sugar 10 minutes on HIGH, covered. Stir to dissolve all the sugar halfway through the cooking time.

3. Stir in orange rind and jelly powder, microwave until boiling and slightly thickened, 2 to 3 minutes on HIGH, uncovered.

4. Pour into jars. Jam will thicken as it cools. Refrigerate.

Yields about 4 cups.

Plum Jam

	boiling water	
2 lbs.	large purple plums	1 kg.
2 cups	sugar	500 mL
1 pkg.	grape jelly powder	85 g

1. Pit plums and place in a 3 quart casserole. Pour just enough boiling water to cover the plums. Microwave uncovered, on HIGH 4–6 minutes. Drain plums and plunge into cold water. Remove and discard skins. Add sugar to plums, mash and microwave on HIGH 6–7 minutes, or until mixture boils rapidly.

2. Add grape jelly powder and stir until dissolved. Pour into prepared jars and set aside to gel.

Yields 3½ cups.

Variation
Use any fresh chopped fruit and corresponding jelly.

Summer Jam

June is a good month to make this jam when fruit is fresh in the stores or garden.

¹/₂ cup	crushed fresh pineapple	125 mL
4 cups	sliced rhubarb (¹/₄ ")	1 L
3 cups	sugar	750 mL
1 cup	mashed fresh strawberries	250 mL
1 tsp.	grated orange rind	5 mL

1. In a large casserole, combine pineapple, rhubarb and sugar. Microwave covered, on HIGH 10 minutes. Stir.

2. Add strawberries and orange rind. Microwave uncovered, on MEDIUM HIGH for 15 to 20 minutes. Pour into jars and refrigerate.

Yields about 4–10 oz. jars of jam.

See photo, page 9.

Amber Jam

The microwave is ideal for making small amounts of jam. If you want a quick gift or a homemade treat for your family, you can make this in less than 30 minutes. Amber Jam has four fresh fruits. Be sure the pineapple is ripe and sweet.

1 cup	diced cantaloupe (about ¹/₂ cantalope)	250 mL
1 cup	diced peaches (approx. 1 large)	250 mL
1 cup	diced fresh pineapple (about ¹/₃ pineapple)	250 mL
1¹/₂ cups	grated firm apples (about 2 medium)	375 mL
2¹/₂ cups	sugar	625 mL

1. In a large 3 qt. (3 L) microwave bowl or casserole, combine all ingredients.

2. Microwave, covered, on HIGH until boiling, approximately 10 minutes. Stir. Microwave uncovered, on HIGH, to desired thickness, approximately 10 minutes. Pour into jars and refrigerate.

Yields approximately 4 cups.

Peach Orange Marmalade

A good way to use peaches when they are so plentiful in the summer. Excellent flavor and color.

2	oranges	2
1/2	lemon	1/2
4 cups	sliced unpeeled peaches	1 L
2 1/2 cups	sugar	625 mL

1. Cut oranges and lemons in half and remove seeds. Grind or grate in a food processor, or chop pulp and slice peel very finely by hand.

2. Place oranges, unpeeled peaches and sugar in a 3 qt. (3 L) microwave pot or casserole. Cover and microwave on HIGH 5 minutes until boiling. Microwave uncovered 15 to 20 minutes MEDIUM HIGH. Pour into jars and let cool. Refrigerate.

Yields 4 cups.

See photo, page 9.

Maple Flavored Pancake Syrup

An easy to make substitute for the real thing!

1/2 cup	butter	125 mL
2/3 cup	brown sugar, packed	150 mL
2 tbsp.	corn syrup	30 mL
1/2 cup	water	125 mL
1/8 tsp.	maple or vanilla flavoring	few drops

1. In a 4 cup measure combine butter, sugar, corn syrup and water. Microwave uncovered, on HIGH 4–5 minutes until syrup is boiling. Add maple flavoring. Butter will rise to the top when refrigerated. Heat and stir before serving.

Yields 1 2/3 cups syrup.

Variation
Tia Maria Pancake Syrup
In place of the 1/2 cup of water use 1/4 cup water and 1/4 cup Tia Maria. This sauce is also excellent poured over cinnamon buns BEFORE baking them in a conventional oven.

Yields approximately 1²/3 cups syrup or enough syrup to cover 12–14 cinnamon buns.

Orange Lemonade Syrup

A refreshing change from canned lemonade. This recipe can easily be doubled.

²/3 cup	sugar	150 mL
1¹/4 cups	water	310 mL
1 tbsp.	grated lemon rind	15 mL
1 cup	freshly squeezed lemon juice (4–5 large lemons)	250 mL
1 tbsp.	grated orange rind	15 mL
1 cup	freshly squeezed orange juice (4–5 large oranges)	250 mL

1. Combine sugar and water. Microwave uncovered, on HIGH for 3 minutes or until sugar is dissolved.

2. Microwave lemons and oranges on HIGH for 1–1¹/2 minutes or until warm. This will help to extract more juice.

3. Add lemon rind, orange rind and juices to syrup. Microwave uncovered, on HIGH an additional 10–12 minutes to blend flavors.

4. Strain syrup and pour into jars. Allow to cool. Cover and refrigerate.

To serve, pour equal amounts of water OR club soda, and fruit syrup over ice. Stir to combine.

Yields 3 cups of syrup.

Candies

Creamy Chocolate Fudge

Smooth and simple. No boil over or messy pots to clean!

1 cup	white sugar	250 mL
1 cup	brown sugar	250 mL
¼ cup	butter	60 mL
¼ cup	corn syrup	60 mL
½ cup	milk	125 mL
2 tbsp.	cocoa	30 mL
1 tsp.	vanilla	5 mL
¼ cup	chopped walnuts	60 mL

1. Grease an 8" (20 cm) pan, and set aside.

2. In an 8 cup (2 L) glass measuring bowl with handle, combine sugars, butter, syrup and milk.

3. Microwave uncovered, on HIGH, two minutes. Stir until well blended and butter is melted.

4. Mix in cocoa and microwave on MEDIUM HIGH 10 to 11 minutes.

5. Remove from microwave, add vanilla and beat on LOW speed with an electric mixer for 5 to 6 minutes, until slightly thickened.

6. Add walnuts and pour into greased pan. Cool.

Yields one pound of fudge.

Variation
For **Vanilla Fudge** Follow the above recipe, omitting cocoa.

Penuche Fudge

A creamy, never fail fudge.

1 cup	brown sugar	250 mL
1/2 cup	margarine	125 mL
1/4 cup	cream or milk	60 mL
1/2 tsp.	vanilla	2 mL
2 cups	sifted powdered sugar	500 mL
1/2 cup	chopped nuts	125 mL

1. Butter a small 5" or 6" (15 cm) square pan.

2. In a 2 qt. (2 L) mixing bowl with handle, measure brown sugar and place margarine on top. Microwave, uncovered, on HIGH 2 to 2½ minutes. Whisk in cream until thoroughly combined. Microwave on HIGH, uncovered 2 to 2½ minutes. Add vanilla and beat with wooden spoon 2 minutes.

2. Add sifted sugar and beat thoroughly until smooth. Add walnuts and pour into prepared pan. Cool before cutting into pieces.

Yields 1 pound of fudge. Approximately 16 pieces.

See photo, page 46.

Variation
For Chocolate Penuche, add ½ cup chocolate chips to melted butter mixture, before whisking in cream in Step 2.

Butter Pecan Fudge

1²/₃ cups	firmly packed brown sugar	400 mL
²/₃ cup	undiluted evaporated milk	150 mL
2 cups	marshmallows	500 mL
1½ cups	butterscotch chips	375 mL
²/₃ cup	chopped pecans	150 mL
1 tsp.	vanilla	5 mL

1. Combine sugar and milk. Microwave on HIGH 1½–2 minutes or until boiling. Boil on HIGH, uncovered for an additional 4–5 minutes.

2. Add marshmallows and butterscotch chips. Microwave on HIGH an additional 30–45 seconds. Stir until marshmallows and chips are melted. Add nuts and vanilla. Pour into a buttered 8×8" square pan. Refrigerate until firm.

Yields approximately 36   1½" squares.

Chocolate Peanut Butter Cups

1 cup	chocolate chips	250 mL
1 cup	mini marshmallows	250 mL
²/₃ cup	peanut butter	150 mL
1 cup	powdered sugar	250 mL
½ cup	chopped peanuts	125 mL
½ cup	evaporated milk	125 mL

1. Combine all ingredients in a 4 cup measure in order given. Micro-wave uncovered, on HIGH 2 minutes or until marshmallows have melted. Stir.

2. Spoon 2 tbsp. of chocolate mixture into small sized double paper muffin liners. Refrigerate until firm.

Yields 18.

Almond Butter Crunch

1 cup	sugar	250 mL
½ cup	corn syrup	125 mL
1 cup	flaked almonds	250 mL
1 tbsp.	butter	15 mL
1 tsp.	almond extract	5 mL
1 tsp.	baking soda	5 mL

1. In an 8 cup glass measure with a handle, combine sugar and corn syrup. Microwave uncovered, on HIGH 4–5 minutes. While syrup is cooking grease a cookie sheet and set aside.

2. Stir in almonds and microwave an additional 3–4 minutes or until syrup just begins to turn a golden color. Add butter and almond extract to syrup. Microwave an additional 1–2 minutes.

3. Add baking soda and gently stir until candy is light and foamy. Pour onto prepared cookie sheet.

Yields approximately 1 lb. See photo, page 45.

Microtip
Grease a wooden spoon BEFORE stirring the candy. This prevents it from sticking to the spoon.

Variation:
For **Peanut Brittle**, substitute peanuts for almonds and vanilla in place of almond extract.

130

Peanut Butter and Prune Chews

These are definitely nutritious.

3 cups	chopped, pitted prunes	750 mL
²/₃ cup	water	150 mL
¹/₃ cup	creamy peanut butter	75 mL
²/₃ cup	finely chopped walnuts	150 mL
²/₃ cup	granola	150 mL
¹/₃ cup	finely chopped peanuts	75 mL

1. In a large bowl combine prunes, water and peanut butter. Microwave uncovered, on HIGH 2–3 minutes, stirring every minute until thickened.

2. Stir in walnuts and granola. Refrigerate for 30 minutes or until completely chilled.

3. Roll into 1 inch round balls and roll each ball into the chopped peanuts. Refrigerate until ready to eat.

Yields approximately 24 prune chews.

Cinnamon Spiced Nuts

Nice to have on hand for that Bridge or Canasta game.

		---:
1	small egg white	1
2 cups	mixed nuts	500 mL
4 tbsp.	brown sugar	60 mL
1 tsp.	cinnamon	5 mL

1. Beat egg white slightly and add nuts, mixing together until nuts are moistened.

2. Combine sugar and cinnamon and mix thoroughly with nuts.

3. Spread evenly over a 9" (23 cm) pie plate. Microwave on HIGH for 3 to 4 minutes, stirring once or twice. Let cool.

Yields 2 cups.

Hawaiian Caramel Corn

A tasty snack treat, similar to commercial Poppycock. Try different variations of fruit and nuts to suit yourself.

8 cups	popped corn	2 L
1 cup	nuts and dried fruit*	250 mL
1 cup	sugar	250 mL
1/3 cup	water	75 mL
1/3 cup	corn syrup	75 mL
1 tsp.	salt	5 mL
1/4 cup	butter or margarine	60 mL

1. In a large buttered pan (a roasting pan is good for this), combine popped corn and mixture of nuts and dried fruits.

2. In an 8 cup (2 L) glass mixing bowl with handle, combine sugar, water, corn syrup, salt and butter. Heat 1 or 2 minutes on HIGH to dissolve sugar. Mix thoroughly.

3. Microwave on HIGH, uncovered, an additional 10 to 12 minutes or until syrup just begins to turn a golden color.

4. Working quickly, pour syrup over popped corn, nuts and fruit. Mix with two greased wooden spoons to thoroughly coat each piece. Press firmly in pan. Let cool before breaking into pieces.

*Use any dried fruit such as pineapple, papaya, banana chips and coconut.

Helpful Hint
A 2 qt. (2 L) glass mixing bowl with **handle** is necessary to make this recipe as the syrup gets very hot.

Caramel Corn

1 cup	brown sugar	250 mL
½ cup	margarine	125 mL
¼ cup	corn syrup	60 mL
½ tsp.	salt	2 mL
½ tsp.	vanilla	2 mL
½ tsp.	baking soda	2 mL
3–4 quarts	popped popcorn	3–4 L

1. In a large glass measuring cup with a handle, combine brown sugar, margarine, corn syrup, salt and vanilla. Microwave uncovered, on HIGH 2–3 minutes or until mixture boils. Boil an additional 1 minute.

2. Remove from microwave, add baking soda, and blend well.

3. Place popcorn in a large bowl, pour syrup over and mix thoroughly. Allow to cool.

Store in a paper bag, or uncovered container.

Butterscotch Candy

½ cup	margarine	125 mL
1 cup	sugar	250 mL
pinch	salt	pinch
¼ cup	corn syrup	60 mL
1 tbsp.	water	15 mL
2 tsp.	vinegar	10 mL

1. Grease an 8″×8″ metal pan. (As metal bends, it will allow easy removal.) In a large glass measure with a handle, combine all the above ingredients.

2. Microwave uncovered for 8–9 minutes or until candy reaches hard ball stage. (This is when candy forms a hard ball when dropped into cold water).

3. Pour candy into pre-greased pan. Allow a few minutes to set and mark into squares. Cool at room temperature and cut with a sharp knife.

Yields approximately 1 lb. of candy.

See photo, page 45.

Slightly Gourmet

Special occasions require special desserts. TRY IT, YOU'LL LIKE IT! shows you how to cook slightly gourmet wth the microwave.

This section of our book is written for those people who don't mind spending a little extra time in the kitchen creating that memorable dessert.

The addition of spirits such as wines or liqueurs will enable you to prepare an elegant dessert that is sure to impress your guests.

Sherry Pudding

This is a light gelatin dessert with a subtle taste of sherry.

2	eggs, separated	2
¹/₂ cup	sugar	125 mL
¹/₂ cup	sherry	125 mL
1 tbsp.	unflavored gelatin	15 mL
¹/₄ cup	water	60 mL
pinch	salt	pinch
¹/₃ cup	sugar	75 mL

1. Combine egg yolks, ¹/₂ cup sugar and sherry. Microwave on MEDIUM 5 to 6 minutes, stirring every minute.

2. Sprinkle gelatin over water in a small dish and microwave 15 to 20 seconds on HIGH until dissolved. Stir.

3. Add gelatin mixture to egg yolks, combing well. Cool, but do not let gelatin set.

4. Beat egg whites with salt until frothy, gradually beating in the ¹/₃ cup sugar until stiff peaks form.

5. Fold cooled custard mixture into the meringue and pour into a greased mold. Chill a few hours to set. Unmold and serve with a Fresh Raspberry or Strawberry Sauce, garnished with a few fresh berries.

See photo, page 100.

Serves 4 to 6.

Amaretto Trifle

Trifle is an excellent dessert served plain or enhanced with the addition of liqueur. Layer trifle in an attractive glass dish so the colorful layers will show through. Starting with plain cake (day old or pound cake is good), and adding jam, fruit and custard, basically completes this versatile dessert. Pat McKinnon shared this recipe with us.

1	small pound cake	1
1/4 cup	Amaretto liqueur	60 mL
2/3 cup	peach jam	150 mL
1/2 cup	toasted slivered almonds	125 mL
14 oz. tin	sliced peaches	398 mL
2 cups	custard	500 mL
	Toasted almonds and whipped cream	
	for garnish	

1. Slice cake evenly and place in bottom of trifle dish. Drizzle with Amaretto. Spread peach jam on top and sprinkle with toasted almonds.

2. Drain peaches thoroughly and place slices around the edge of the dish. Pour custard over all and refrigerate 4 hours or over night. Top with whipped cream and a few toasted almonds.

Custard

2 cups	whole milk	500 mL
4	eggs	4
1/3 cup	sugar	75 mL
1 tbsp.	cornstarch	15 mL
2 tbsp.	Amaretto liqueur	30 mL

1. In the microwave, bring milk just to the boil (scald), 4 to 5 minutes on HIGH.

2. In a 2 qt. (2 L) measure, beat eggs, sugar and cornstarch together and slowly beat in hot milk. Microwave on MEDIUM, 6 to 7 minutes until slightly thickened and mixture coats the back of a spooon. Whisk until smooth. Stir in Amaretto.

Microtip
In place of pound cake, use Yellow Cake page .

See photo, page 100.

Old Fashioned Vanilla Ice Cream

I scream, You scream for Old Fashioned Ice Cream!

½ cup	sugar	125 mL
3 tbsp.	flour	45 mL
1¼ cups	milk	310 mL
1	egg yolk, beaten	1
⅛ tsp.	salt	pinch
1	egg white, stiffly beaten	1
1½ cups	whipping cream	375 mL
2 tsp.	vanilla	10 mL

1. In a large bowl combine sugar and flour. Whisk in milk. Micro-wave uncovered, on HIGH 3–4 minutes or until slightly thickened, stirring once or twice.

2. Stir a little hot mixture into the beaten egg yolk, and return to the remaining hot mixture. Whisk well and cool completely.

3. Fold stiffly beaten egg white into cooled custard. Place in freezer for 1 hour or until completely chilled but not frozen.

4. Whip cream with vanilla and fold into chilled custard. Cover and place in freezer until completely frozen. About 2–3 hours.

Yields 5 cups of rich creamy ice-cream.

Top with any of our delicious sauces.

A whisk incorporates more air into the egg whites making them higher and lighter. Best whipped at room temperature. To bring egg whites to room temperature, heat 5 or 6 seconds in the microwave.

Fresh Fruit Ring

A light creamy frozen dessert. Great with any fruit.

1 cup	white sugar	250 mL
1/3 cup	water	75 mL
1/8 tsp.	cream of tartar	pinch
2	egg whites	2
2 tsp.	vanilla	10 mL
pinch	salt	pinch
	food coloring, optional	
1 cup	whipping cream, whipped	250 mL
1 cup	fresh fruit, chopped	250 mL
	fresh fruit for garnish	

1. Combine sugar, water and cream of tartar in a large glass bowl. Microwave on HIGH 3½ to 4½ minutes or until the syrup reaches the soft ball stage. Syrup forms a ball when a small amount is dropped into a glass of cold water.

2. While syrup is cooking, whip egg whites until frothy. Add vanilla, salt and food coloring. Beat until stiff peaks form.

3. When syrup is done, SLOWLY pour it into the beaten egg whites, beating continuously for 2 to 3 minutes or until stiff.

4. Fold whipped cream into egg white mixture. Fold in 1 cup chopped fruit. Pour into a two quart jelly mold. Freeze for 2–3 hours or until firm.

5. Unmold and decorate center with an assortment of fresh fruit. See cover photo.

Baked Custard

1³/₄ cups	milk	425 mL
¹/₄ cup	sugar	60 mL
3	eggs	3
¹/₄ tsp.	salt	1 mL
¹/₂ tsp.	vanilla	2 mL
	nutmeg	

1. Combine milk, sugar, eggs, salt, and vanilla in a shallow 1 quart casserole dish.

2. Sprinkle with nutmeg and microwave uncovered on DEFROST for 15 minutes, then on MEDIUM HIGH for an additional 4 to 6 minutes or until knife comes out clean when inserted in center. Spoon into 4 dessert dishes and serve with sauce or fruit.

Serves 4.

Variation
Creme Caramel

¹/₂ cup	sugar	125 mL
¹/₂ cup	water	125 mL
1	Baked Custard Recipe	1

1. Combine sugar and water in a 1 quart shallow dish. Microwave uncovered on HIGH 10–13 minutes or until syrup turns a deep golden color.

2. Remove approximately 2–3 tbsp. of syrup and drizzle it onto a greased cookie sheet. Allow to harden and use as a garnish over your Creme Caramel.

3. Combine custard ingredients, omitting nutmeg. Pour uncooked custard through a strainer into the 1 qt. shallow dish over syrup.

4. Microwave covered on MEDIUM LOW 15–16 minutes then on MEDIUM HIGH for an additional 2–3 minutes or until knife inserted in centre comes out clean. Allow to cool completely before turning out onto a serving dish.

5. Remove hardened syrup from cookie sheet, crush and sprinkle it over custard.

Queen of Bread Pudding

This is a real old English favorite, updated for the microwave.

5 slices	white bread	5
1/3 cup	butter	75 mL
1/3 cup	sugar	75 mL
2 tsp.	grated lemon rind	10 mL
2 tbsp.	lemon juice	30 mL
1 cup	milk	250 mL
1	egg	1
2	eggs, separated	2
1/4 cup	raspberry jam	60 mL
1 tbsp.	sugar	15 mL
few drops	red food coloring	few drops

1. Trim crusts off bread and cut into cubes.

2. In a large mixing bowl, melt butter on HIGH 30 to 40 seconds.

3. Combine bread, melted butter, sugar, lemon rind and juice in a microwave safe attractive 6 cup (1.5 L) serving bowl, with no silver or gold trim.

4. Beat together milk, 1 whole egg and 2 egg yolks. Pour over bread mixture. Microwave, covered, on HIGH 6 to 8 minutes.

5. Spread raspberry jam evenly over cooked pudding.

6. Beat remaining 2 egg whites until frothy. Add sugar and red food coloring and beat until stiff. Spoon on top of jam, covering completely with meringue. Microwave on HIGH 30 to 40 seconds.

Bananas Marakesh

This is a very popular dessert, served at the Naam Restaurant, in Vancouver. We thank them for sharing it with us. A very easy, elegant dessert made in minutes. Should be cooled before serving.

¹/₂ cup	dates	125 mL
¹/₂ cup	water	125 mL
1 tsp.	lemon juice	5 mL
4 to 5	bananas	4 to 5
1 cup	whipping cream	250 mL
1 tbsp.	sugar	15 mL
	allspice	

1. Combine dates, water and lemon juice. Microwave on HIGH, covered, 1 to 2 minutes until mushy, stir to blend.

2. Place a layer of evenly sliced bananas (¹/₂″ thick) in the bottom of a 9″ (23 cm) pie or quiche pan.

3. Spread date filling over top of bananas. Top with another layer of sliced bananas.

4. Whip cream with sugar and pile evenly over all. Sprinkle with allspice. Refrigerate until ready to serve.

See photo, page 82.

Yields approximately 6 to 8 servings.

Variation
In place of dates, try an apricot filling.

Apricot Filling

1 cup	chopped dried apricots	250 mL
1¹/₄ cups	water	310 mL
1 tsp.	lemon juice	5 mL
1 tbsp.	sugar	15 mL

Microwave all ingredients on HIGH, covered, 2 minutes. Puree in blender or food processor.

This dessert may also be served in a cooked pastry crust.

Watermelon Sorbet

A sorbet is a light, refreshing change from heavier desserts. It may be served between courses to clear the palate.

⅓ cup	water	75 mL
⅓ cup	sugar	75 mL
1½ cups	pureed, seeded watermelon	375 mL
1 tsp.	finely grated lemon rind	5 mL
1 tbsp.	lemon juice	15 mL
2 tbsp.	rum	30 mL

1. In a 4 cup measure combine sugar and water. Microwave uncovered on HIGH 1½–2 minutes or until boiling. Boil one additional minute, stirring to dissolve sugar. Place in fridge until completely cooled, about 1 hour.

2. Add cooled syrup to watermelon puree. Whisk in lemon rind, juice and rum. Pour mixture into a loaf pan, cover with foil and freeze until partly frozen, about 1 hour, whisk each ½ hour.

3. Beat egg whites until stiff and whisk into partially frozen puree. Return to freezer, whisking 3–4 times for approximately 4 hours. Spoon into 4 parfait or sherbert glasses before serving. Garnish with a thin triangle of watermelon.

Serves 4.

Variation
In place of watermelon puree, use any pureed fruit such as honey dew melon or canteloupe. When using pureed strawberries or raspberries strain the seeds.

For a tangier taste, use citrus juices in place of pureed fruit.

See photo, page 82.

Dessert Crepe Batter

Although crepes cannot be cooked in the microwave, they transform fruit and sauces into elegant desserts in minutes. Make a batch and have on hand in the freezer.

3	large eggs	3
1½ cups	milk	375 mL
3 tbsp.	melted butter	45 mL
1 cup	all purpose flour	250 mL
3 tbsp.	sugar	45 mL
¼ cup	orange flavored liqueur or brandy	60 mL

1. Combine all ingredients in a blender or food processor and blend until smooth.

2. Pour batter into a container, cover and refrigerate at least 2 hours. The batter may be kept for a week in the refrigerator.

3. Brush a crepe pan with a little butter and heat until the pan is hot enough to 'sizzle' a drop of water.

4. Pour in just enough crepe batter to cover bottom of pan, tilting the pan to help swirl batter over the bottom. Cook about 1 minute over medium high heat until golden brown on the bottom. It is not necessary to brown the other side.

5. As the crepes are baked, stack them in a pie plate and cover to keep from drying out. Cook only as many as needed or finish the batter and freeze.

Yields approximately 12 to 18, depending on size of crepe pan.

Pineapple Filling For Crepes

¼ cup	butter	60 mL
¼ cup	sugar	60 mL
14 oz. tin	pineapple tidbits	398 mL
1 tbsp.	orange brandy	15 mL
1 tbsp.	cornstarch	15 mL
1 cup	whipping cream, whipped	250 mL

1. In a 1 qt. (1 L) mixing bowl, combine all ingredients except whipping cream and microwave on MEDIUM 5 to 6 minutes or until slightly thickened, stirring once or twice.

2. Place about ¼ cup filling down the center of each crepe. Roll crepes over filling and top with whipped cream.

Yields 2 cups of filling. Enough for 8 crepes.

Orange Filling For Crepes

¼ cup	butter	60 mL
¼ cup	sugar	60 mL
½ cup	orange juice	125 mL
2	large oranges peeled, (white portion removed), seeded and chopped	2
1 tsp.	lemon rind	5 mL
1½ tbsp.	orange liqueur	22 mL
1½ tbsp.	cornstarch	22 mL
1 cup	whipping cream, whipped	250 mL
	toasted flaked almonds for garnish	

1. Microwave butter, sugar and orange juice on HIGH 2 minutes. Stir. Add chopped oranges, lemon rind and liqueur.

2. Mix cornstarch with a little juice and blend into orange mixture.

3. Microwave MEDIUM 5 to 6 minutes. Stir two or three times. Place ¼ cup filling down the center of each crepe and roll crepe over filling. Reheat a few seconds if serving warm. Top with whipped cream.

Yields 2 cups of filling — enough for 8 crepes.

See Dessert Crepe batter page 142.

Zucchini Fruit Cake

We have made this instead of the 'traditional' fruit cake at Christmas. It has the appearance and flavor of a medium dark cake. Make it 2 weeks ahead, so it will have time to mellow.

2	eggs	2
³/₄ cup	oil	175 mL
1 cup	brown sugar	250 mL
¹/₂ tbsp.	vanilla	7 mL
1¹/₂ cups	flour	375 mL
¹/₂ tbsp.	cinnamon	7 mL
1 tsp.	allspice	5 mL
¹/₂ tsp.	nutmeg	2 mL
¹/₂ tsp.	cloves	2 mL
1 tsp.	baking soda	5 mL
¹/₂ tsp.	salt	2 mL
¹/₂ tsp.	baking powder	2 mL
1 cup	peeled and shredded zucchini	250 mL
1 cup	chopped walnuts	250 mL
1 cup	raisins	250 mL
¹/₂ cup	currants	125 mL
1 cup	chopped glazed fruit	250 mL
¹/₄ cup	brandy	60 mL

1. In a large microwave safe mixing bowl, beat eggs, oil, brown sugar and vanilla well.

2. In a separate bowl, combine flour, cinnamon, allspice, nutmeg, cloves, soda, salt and baking powder.

3. Mix dry ingredients into wet and stir until thoroughly combined.

4. Blend in zucchini, walnuts, raisins, currant and fruit.

5. Before putting batter in a bundt pan, microwave it in the mixing bowl 5 minutes on HIGH, STIRRING EVERY MINUTE. (This helps the batter become warm throughout and will produce a more evenly cooked cake.)

6. Spoon warm batter into a large 12 cup (3 L) microwave bundt pan. Microwave covered, 5 to 6 minutes on HIGH.

7. Puncture top of cake with a small skewer and drizzle with brandy. Allow to cool. Wrap completely and store in the refrigerator 2 weeks before serving.

Yields 1 cake.

Chocolate Zucchini Cake

A large dark chocolate cake, using some of the zucchini you have in your garden. It is not necessary to peel the zucchini before shredding.

2 cups	flour	500 mL
1 tsp.	baking powder	5 mL
1 tsp.	baking soda	5 mL
1 tbsp.	instant coffee granules	15 mL
¹/₂ tsp.	salt	2 mL
¹/₂ cup	cocoa	125 mL
3	eggs	3
2 cups	white sugar	500 mL
²/₃ cup	oil	150 mL
¹/₃ cup	sour milk*	75 mL
2 cups	finely shredded zucchini	500 mL
1 tsp.	vanilla	5 mL
1 cup	chopped walnuts	250 mL

1. In a large mixing bowl, combine, flour, baking powder, soda, coffee, salt and cocoa.

2. In a separate bowl, beat eggs, sugar, oil and sour milk. Blend into dry ingredients. Add zucchini, vanilla and walnuts.

3. Spoon batter into a 12 cup microwave bundt pan. Microwave on HIGH 10 to 12 minutes. Let stand 10 minutes before turning out. Frost with your favorite frosting

*If sour milk is not available, add 1 tsp. lemon juice or vinegar to whole milk. Let stand 2 to 3 minutes.

Yields 1 large cake.

Variation
For extra chocolate flavor, add 1 cup chocolate chips in place of the walnuts.

Praline Tea Cakes

A delightful little tea cake iced with a creamy lemon frosting, and topped with home made praline.

Praline Crunch

¹/₂ cup	sugar	125 mL
¹/₃ cup	hot tap water	75 mL
¹/₃ cup	chopped pecans	75 mL

1. Combine sugar and water in a large glass measuring cup or bowl. Microwave uncovered, on HIGH for 7–8 minutes or until the sugar JUST begins to turn a pale golden color. (Watch carefully as this can burn quickly).

2. Sprinkle the pecans into a greased 8″×8″ (20 cm) metal pan. Pour hot syrup over top, spreading it out as evenly as possible. Set aside to cool at room temperature.

3. When completely hardened break the Praline into fairly small pieces, but not to a fine powder. Set aside.

Lemon Tea Cakes

1¹/₃ cups	flour	325 mL
2 tsp.	baking powder	10 mL
¹/₂ cup	sugar	125 mL
¹/₄ tsp.	salt	1 mL
¹/₂ cup	butter	125 mL
2	eggs	2
¹/₃ cup	lemon juice	75 mL
¹/₂ cup	warm tap water	125 mL

1. In a large mixing bowl combine flour, baking powder, sugar and salt. Cut in butter until mixture is crumbly.

2. In a separate bowl combine eggs, lemon juice, and water. Combine egg mixture with the dry ingredients. Stir until smooth.

3. Place 6 large muffin liners in a microwave muffin pan. Fill each two thirds full. Microwave covered 1¹/₂–2¹/₂ minutes on HIGH. Place Tea Cakes on rack to cool (Repeat with remaining batter.) Spread Butter Cream Frosting over each cake. Garnish with praline crunch.

Yields 12 tea cakes.

If you do not have a microwave muffin pan, cut off the top half of paper or styrofoam cups and line with the muffin paper liner. Place 6 in a shallow dish. Follow directions according to recipe.

Lemon Butter Cream Frosting

³/₄ cup	soft butter	175 mL
³/₄ cup	powdered sugar	175 mL
1	egg yolk	1
¹/₃ cup	lemon juice	75 ml

1. Combine above ingredients and beat until creamy.

Yields enough frosting for 12 tea cakes.

Upside–down Black Forest Cake

A quick way to impress last minute quests!

1 – 8 oz.	single layer chocolake cake mix	227 g
1 cup	cherry pie filling	250 mL
1 tsp.	grated lemon rind	5 mL
2 tsp.	cherry brandy or kirsch	10 mL
	whip cream and shaved chocolate for garnish	

1. Mix cake according to package directions. Set aside.

2. In a 8" (20 cm) microwave cake pan combine cherry pie filling, lemon rind and brandy. Microwave on HIGH for 1 minute or until heated through.

3. Pour cake batter evenly over top of heated cherries. Cover and microwave on HIGH 4–5 minutes. Let stand 5 minutes, loosen sides with spatula and carefully invert onto a serving platter.

Garnish with 1 cup sweetened whipped cream, and shaved chocolate.

Tip
If you don't have a mix handy, see page 15 for a one layer chocolate cake.

Icelandic Vinertarta

This is an Icelandic "Celebration" cake. Traditionally made for Christmas, birthdays or whenever a special cake was needed. Chris Stewart, a friend of Joyce's, was famous among her family and friends for her Vinertarta. This is her original recipe.

For cake

1 cup	butter	250 mL
1½ cups	white sugar	375 mL
2	large eggs	2
2 tbsp.	cream	30 mL
2 tsp.	almond extract	10 mL
4 cups	flour	1 L
1 tsp.	baking powder	5 mL

1. In a large mixing bowl, cream butter, and add sugar gradually. Add eggs, one at a time, beating after each addition. Blend in cream and almond extract.

2. Sift flour and baking powder together. Work flour into the butter mixture.

3. Divide dough into 5 equal parts. Approximately ½ pound (250 g) each.

4. Line a 9", (23 cm) cake or quiche pan with wax paper. Lightly flour. Press one part of dough into the pan evenly.

5. Microwave uncovered, on HIGH 3 to 3½ minutes. Remove from pan, place on a rack to cool and carefully peel off wax paper. Repeat with remaining dough.

Filling

1 lb.	pitted prunes	454 g
2 cups	water	500 mL
1 cup	white sugar	250 g
1 tbsp.	cinnamon	15 mL
1 tsp.	vanilla	5 mL

1. In a large mixing bowl, combine pitted prunes and water. Cover and microwave on HIGH 10 to 12 minutes until prunes are soft.

2. Beat prunes until mushy and add sugar, cinnamon and vanilla. Let cool. Filling should be fairly thick.

To Assemble

1. Place one crust on a plate and layer with one quarter of the filling, approximately 1 cup.

2. Repeat with remaining crusts and filling. Ice top only with a thin butter icing. This cake should be allowed to stand for 2 to 3 weeks before serving. It may be frozen.

Butter Icing

6 tbsp.	butter	90 mL
1½ cups	powdered sugar	375 mL
¼ tsp.	almond extract	2 mL
1	egg yolk	1

1. Place all ingredients in a mixing bowl and beat until creamy and light. Spread on top of Vinertarta.

2. Cut in slices as you would for Christmas cake, not wedges. See cover photo.

Chocolate Fondue

This was such a popular dessert a few years back, but still is a nice treat as a 'dipping' sauce when serving fresh fruit. Bananas and strawberries are particularly attractive served this way.

1 cup	chocolate chips	250 mL
¼ cup	cream	60 mL
¼ cup	corn syrup	60 mL
1 tsp.	vanilla	5 mL
pinch	salt	pinch
1 tbsp.	liqueur of your choice	15 mL

1. In a 2 cup measure, melt chocolate chips on MEDIUM HIGH, 2 minutes. Stir in remaining ingredients and microwave on MEDIUM 3 to 4 minutes. Add liqueur and stir with whisk until well blended and smooth.

Yields about 1½ cups.

Velvet Hammer Pie

A cocktail with the combination of Cointreau and Kahlua gave this pie its name. Try any combination of liqueurs and create your own favorite pie!

Crust

¹/₃ cup	melted butter	75 mL
1¹/₂ cups	graham wafer crumbs	375 mL
2 tbsp.	cocoa	30 mL
¹/₃ cup	powdered sugar	75 mL

Filling

¹/₂ cup	water	125 mL
1 tbsp.	unflavored gelatin	15 mL
3	eggs, separated	3
¹/₃ cup	sugar	75 mL
¹/₄ cup	Cointreau	60 mL
¹/₄ cup	Kahlua	60 mL
¹/₄ tsp.	cream of tartar	1 mL
1 cup	whipping cream	250 mL
1 tbsp.	powdered sugar	15 mL
2 tbsp.	Cointreau	30 mL
	Chocolate curls	

1. For crust combine melted butter, graham wafer crumbs, cocoa and powdered sugar in a mixing bowl. Press evenly into the bottom of a 9″ (23 cm) pie or quiche pan. Microwave uncovered, 45 seconds to 1 minute. Set aside.

2. Sprinkle gelatin over water in a one cup measure. Microwave uncovered, on HIGH 30 seconds to dissolve gelatin. Stir and set aside.

3. Beat egg yolks well. Add sugar and continue to beat until thick and light in color, approximately 2 minutes.

4. Add gelatin, Cointreau and Kahlua to egg yolk mixture and microwave on MEDIUM for 3 to 4 minutes, stirring every minute until slightly thickened. Allow to cool, but not set. (approximately ¹/₂ hour.)

5. Beat egg whites until light and fluffy. Add cream of tartar, beating until stiff peaks form.

6. In a separate bowl, whip cream until thick, add powdered sugar, and remaining 2 tablespoons of Cointreau. Fold egg whites and whipping cream into egg yolk mixture.Pour into cooked pie crust. Refrigerate until set. Garnish with whipped cream and chocolate curls.

Petits Fours

These dainty little cakes make a nice addition to a dessert tray. Color the coconut in different shades for an attractive arrangement. Cake should be made a day in advance.

1 pkg.	small yellow cake mix	250 g

1. Make cake according to package directions. Microwave half the batter in a 2 cup (500 mL) loaf pan, 2 minutes on HIGH. Repeat with remaining batter. Let cake stand one day.

Butter Icing

¹/₂ cup	butter	125 mL
1 cup	powdered sugar	250 mL
1 tsp.	grated lemon rind	5 mL
1 tsp.	grated orange rind	5 mL
	orange juice	
2 cups	dessicated coconut	500 mL
	food coloring	

1. Beat butter until creamy. Add powdered sugar, lemon rind, orange rind and enough orange juice to make a spreading consistency.

2. Cut cooled cake into 1¹/₂" cubes. Ice all sides and roll in tinted coconut.

Yields one dozen.

Microtip
If icing is too stiff, microwave 10 to 15 seconds. Hold cake cubes with a fork while icing.

Make Yellow Cake for One or Two (Page 16) in place of cake mix.

Nesselrode Pie

It is believed this recipe was developed for Count Nesselrode of Russia in the Early 1800's. It was originally a pudding using chestnut puree, glaced cherries and candied orange peel. Because of the color combination, this would be elegant served as part of the holiday buffet.

Crumb Crust

1¹/₄ cups	graham cracker crumbs	310 mL
3 tbsp.	cocoa	45 mL
¹/₄ cup	sugar	60 mL
¹/₄ cup	melted butter	60 mL

1. Combine all crust ingredients and mix thoroughly. Pat firmly onto bottom and sides of a 9" (23 cm) quiche or pie pan. Microwave 1 to 1¹/₂ minutes on HIGH, uncovered. Set in refrigerator until cool.

Filling

3	eggs, separated	3
¹/₂ cup	sugar	125 mL
1 cup	milk	250 mL
1 tbsp.	unflavored gelatin	15 mL
¹/₄ cup	rum	60 mL
1 small tin	Chestnut Puree*	250 g
¹/₂ cup	chopped glaced cherries	125 mL
¹/₄ tsp.	cream of tartar	1 mL
¹/₄ cup	sugar	60 mL
1 cup	whipping cream	250 mL
	chocolate curls and whipped cream for garnish	

1. Beat egg yolks lightly and add ¹/₂ cup sugar. Continue beating until well blended. Add milk and mix thoroughly. Microwave on MEDIUM HIGH 5 to 6 minutes, stirring every minute. Custard should be slightly thickened, but not curdled. (If it does curdle, strain the custard.) Cool custard in ice water approximately 20 minutes, stirring occasionally.

2. In a small bowl combine gelatin and rum. Microwave 20 seconds on HIGH to soften gelatin. Set Aside.

3. Add chestnut puree, chopped cherries and gelatin mixture to cooled custard.

4. Beat egg whites with cream of tartar, add the ¼ cup sugar, 1 tbsp. at a time beating until stiff peaks form.

5. Whip the cream. Fold egg whites and whipped cream into the cooled, half–set custard. Blend thoroughly and pour into cooled pie crust. Chill several hours or overnight. Garnish with chocolate curls and whipped cream.

See photo, page 64.

Serves 8.

*Chestnut Puree or Chestnut Sauce (Nesselrode), a blend of chestnuts, fruit and rum, may be purchased in some food stores or specialty shops. If it is hard to find you may substitute 1 cup thoroughly drained crushed pineapple.

Rich Lemon Butter Tarts

Joyce's mother–in–law's mother won a prize for her lemon tarts, many years ago with this recipe.

3	eggs	3
1 cup	sugar	250 mL
	zest* of 1 lemon	
	juice of 2 lemons, approx. ⅓ cup	75 mL

1. Mix together all ingredients in a 4 cup (1 L) mixing bowl. Microwave on MEDIUM, 5 to 6 minutes or until thickened, stirring 2 or 3 times. Cool. Cover and store in refrigerator.

Yields enough for about 12 tarts.

Helpful Hint
*The zest of a lemon is only the very outer layer of the peel.

Heat lemon 15 seconds in the microwave before extracting juice.

See photo, page 64.

Double Chocolate Mousse Pie

For a delicious dessert to complete an elegant meal, try this easy to make pie. It has a layer of chocolate between crust and filling!

1 – 9"	Graham Cracker chocolate crumb crust	23 cm
½ cup	semi–sweet chocolate chips	125 mL
1 tbsp.	butter or margarine	15 mL
1 tbsp.	milk	15 mL
⅓ cup	chocolate chips	75 mL
1 cup	milk	250 mL
⅓ cup	sugar	75 mL
1 tbsp.	unflavored gelatin	15 mL
1 tbsp.	chocolate or coffee flavored liqueur	15 mL
3	egg whites	3
pinch	salt	pinch
	whipped cream and chocolate curls to garnish	

1. Prepare crumb crust (page 85) and set aside to cool.

2. Microwave ½ cup chocolate chips, butter and milk in a 1 cup measure on HIGH 40 to 50 seconds. Stir until smooth. Pour over cooled crumb crust.

3. Combine ⅓ cup chocolate chips and 1 cup milk. Microwave on HIGH 2 minutes, until chocolate has melted. Stir, add sugar, gelatin and liqueur.

4. Microwave on HIGH 1 minute, stir to blend. Microwave an additional 3 minutes on MEDIUM, whisking every minute. Cool.

5. Beat egg whites and salt together until stiff. Add cooled chocolate mixture and combine thoroughly. Pour into crumb crust over chocolate layer and cool until set.

6. Decorate with whipping cream and chocolate curls.

Variation
Use different liqueurs of your choice. Amaretto, Triple Sec and white Creme de Menthe, to name a few. Add ¼ cup finely chopped nuts to crumb crust for more "crunch".

Prune Whips

These tarts have been a tradition in the Webster family for years. Although traditionally made at Christmas, they are a treat all year round. Make the filling and keep covered in the refrigerator. Assemble tarts as needed.

> Cooked Pastry Tart Shells
> Prune Filling
> Whipped Cream for Topping

Prune Filling

2 cups	pitted prunes	500 mL
³/₄ cup	water	175 mL
¹/₄ cup	sugar	60 mL
1 tbsp.	lemon juice	15 mL
¹/₄ tsp.	cardamom	1 mL

1. In a 4 cup (1 L) microwave measure, combine prunes and water. Microwave HIGH, covered, 3 to 4 minutes. Stir in sugar, lemon juice and cardamom. Puree in food processor or blender. Cool before filling tart shells. Top with whipped cream.

See photo, page 64.

Yields approximately 2¹/₂ cups filling.

Variation
Prune Whip Parfait

2 cups	prune filling (above)	500 mL
2	egg whites	2
pinch	salt	pinch
¹/₄ cup	sugar	60 mL
¹/₂ cup	whipping cream, whipped	125 mL

1. Beat egg whites and salt together until foamy. Add sugar gradually and beat until stiff peaks form.

2. Fold prune filling into stiffly beaten egg whites one quarter at a time until thoroughly blended. Fold in half the whipped cream. Spoon into 6 or 8 parfait glasses. Cool.

3. Just before serving, garnish with dollops of remaining whipped cream.

Yields 6 to 8 servings.

Apricot Honey Butter Cheesecake

You will get rave reviews for this one. How clever of you to have made the Apricot Honey Butter too!

Crust

1 cup	graham cracker crumbs	250 mL
¼ cup	finely chopped walnuts	60 mL
¼ cup	brown sugar	60 mL
¼ cup	melted butter	60 mL

Filling

12 oz.	cream cheese	350 g
2	eggs	2
1 cup	Apricot Honey Butter, divided (page 122)	250 mL
2 tsp.	lemon juice	10 mL
2 tbsp.	sugar	30 mL

1. For the crust, thoroughly combine graham crumbs, walnuts, brown sugar and melted butter. Save ¼ cup crumbs for topping and pat the rest into a 9″ (23 cm) quiche or pie pan. Microwave on HIGH 1 to 1½ minutes. Set aside.

2. In a large mixing bowl, soften cream cheese on HIGH 20 or 30 seconds. Mix in eggs, ¾ cup Apricot Honey Butter, lemon juice and sugar.

3. Microwave on MEDIUM HIGH, 6 to 7 minutes, whisking every minute. Pour into baked crumb crust. Microwave 1 to 2 minutes on MEDIUM HIGH.

4. Warm remaining ¼ cup Apricot Honey Butter, 20 seconds on HIGH and glaze top of cheesecake. Sprinkle ¼ cup crumbs in a spiral fashion over all.

Yield 1 – 9″ cheesecake.

Champagne Jelly

Champagne Jelly is a particularly appreciated gift. Have some on hand for that special person.

4 cups	champagne	1 L
4 cups	sugar	1 L
³/₄ cup	liquid pectin	175 mL

1. In a 3 quart casserole, combine champagne and sugar. Microwave uncovered on HIGH 10–12 minutes or until mixture begins to boil rapidly. Stir to dissolve sugar. Bring to boil for an additional 2 minutes.

2. Add pectin gradually into boiling mixture, pour into prepared, attractive jelly glasses.

Yields approximately 5½ cups.

See photo, page 9.

Sangria Jelly

2 cups	sangria wine	500 mL
2½ cups	sugar	625 mL
6	whole cloves	6
2	large cinnamon sticks	2
2 – 2 inch	strips orange peel	2
6 tbsp.	liquid pectin	90 mL

1. In a large measure combine wine, sugar, cloves, cinnamon and orange peel.

2. Microwave uncovered, on HIGH 3–4 minutes or until sugar has completely dissolved. Stir and microwave an additional 3 minutes or until the wine comes to a full rolling boil.

3. Strain and add pectin. Stir and pour into sterilized glass jars. Seal with lid or melted paraffin wax.

Yields 4 cups tasty jelly!

Chocolate Brandy Balls

Not too sweet.

1 cup	vanilla or graham wafer crumbs	250 mL
1/3 cup	brandy	75 mL
1 cup	chocolate chips	250 mL
2 tbsp.	margarine or butter	30 mL
1/3 cup	finely chopped walnuts or pecans	75 mL
1½ cups	powdered sugar, approximately	375 mL

1. In a bowl, combine crumbs and brandy. Set aside.

2. Place chocolate chips and butter in a 2 cup measure. Microwave on HIGH 1 minute or until chips have melted. Stir until smooth.

3. Pour melted chocolate into crumb mixture. Add chopped nuts and JUST ENOUGH POWDERED SUGAR to make a soft dough. Shape into 1" (2.5 cm) round balls. Cool slightly and coat with remaining sugar. Roll in coconut (optional).

Yields approximately 46 balls.

Chocolate Rum Truffles

4 – 1 oz.	squares semi–sweet chocolate	125 g
1/4 cup	butter	60 mL
3 tbsp.	dark rum	45 mL
1/2 cup	powdered sugar	125 mL
1/2 cup	ground almonds	125 mL
2 tbsp.	cocoa	30 mL
1 tbsp.	powdered sugar	30 mL

1. In a 4 cup measure, place chocolate, butter and rum. Microwave uncovered on HIGH 1–2 minutes or until completely melted. Stir at least once.

2. Add powdered sugar and ground almonds to melted chocolate, combine well. Place in refrigerator for 30 minutes to completely cool, or until mixture is chilled enough to form into balls.

3. In a separate measure, combine cocoa and sugar. Form 12 – 1" round balls with the chilled chocolate and coat in cocoa/sugar mixture. Refrigerate.

See photo, page 45.

Yields 12 truffles.

Sugared Orange Peel

This is a flavorful attractive confection. Dip some in melted chocolate for an added treat. This is also good with lemon rind.

3	large oranges	3
	water	
1¹/₂ cups	sugar, divided	375 mL
¹/₂ cup	water	125 mL

1. Divide oranges into sections and carefully peel each section.

2. Place peel in a 4 cup measure and add enough water to cover. Microwave on HIGH covered until boiling. Boil about 5 minutes. Drain water and repeat boiling and draining process two more times. After last draining, scrape part of the white from the peel. Cut peel into ¹/₄ inch strips. Set aside.

3. In a mixing bowl with handle, combine 1 cup of sugar and water. Microwave on MEDIUM 2 minutes, or until sugar is dissolved. Stir. Microwave, covered, on HIGH 5 minutes. Remove cover and microwave an additional 3 minutes on HIGH until syrup forms a thread when dropped from a spoon.

4. Add orange strips to syrup and microwave on MEDIUM LOW 15 minutes, stirring once or twice.

5. Place wax paper under racks and spread peel over top of racks to cool slightly. Sprinkle a few pieces at a time in the remaining ¹/₂ cup of sugar.

6. When cool, dip strips into melted chocolate if desired.

See photo, page 45.

Brandy Cream Sauce

A delicate sauce to enhance almost any dessert.

½ cup	sugar	125 mL
½ cup	water	125 mL
pinch	salt	pinch
2	egg yolks	2
2 tbsp.	brandy	30 mL
½ cup	whipping cream, whipped	125 mL

1. In a 4 cup (1 L) mixing bowl, combine sugar, water and salt. Microwave on HIGH 7 to 8 minutes, or until a syrup consistency.

2. In a separate bowl, beat egg yolks and add brandy. Pour boiling syrup into the egg mixture, beating constantly with an electric mixer. Cool.

3. Fold whipped cream into cooled brandy mixture.

Yields about 1½ cups.

Variations
Use your choice of liqueur in place of brandy to serve with different fruits.

Use orange liqueur to serve with strawberries
     chocolate liqueur to serve with bananas
     almond liqueur to serve with pears
     brandy to serve with peaches

Rich and Creamy Chocolate Sauce

A true chocolate sauce, expensive but worth it

1 cup	heavy cream	250 mL
8 oz.	good quality semi–sweet chocolate, cut up	250 g

1. Bring cream just to the boil, about 2 minutes on HIGH. Blend in chocolate until melted. Add 1 minute on MEDIUM to finish melting chocolate if necessary.

Yields about 2 cups sauce.

Amaretto Applesauce

This sauce is fabulous over Gingerbread!

4	apples, peeled and cored	4
2 tbsp.	butter	30 mL
1/2 cup	sugar	125 mL
1 tsp.	grated orange rind	5 mL
2 tbsp.	orange juice	30 mL
1	egg, separated	1
2 tbsp.	Amaretto Liquor	30 mL

1. Chop apples and combine with butter, sugar, orange rind and juice in a 4 cup (1 L) mixing bowl. Microwave on HIGH 5 minutes, uncovered. Stirring once or twice. Puree apples in food processor or blender.

2. Beat egg yolk and Amaretto together. Add to applesauce.

3. Whip egg white until stiff. Gradually blend in applesauce.

Yields 2 cups sauce.

Creme De Menthe Frosting

1/3 cup	butter	75 mL
1 1/2 cups	powdered sugar	375 mL
1 tbsp.	corn syrup	15 mL
2 tbsp.	Creme de Menthe Liqueur	30 mL
1/2 tsp.	vanilla	2 mL

Chocolate Glaze

1/2 cup	chocolate chips	125 mL
1 tbsp.	butter	15 mL
1 tbsp.	milk	15 mL

1. In a 4 cup measure combine butter, sugar, corn syrup, Creme de Menthe and vanilla. Stir until smooth and creamy.

2. In a separate measure combine chocolate chips and butter. Microwave uncovered, on HIGH 1 minute or until chocolate has melted. Stir in milk until smooth.

3. Spread Creme de Menthe frosting over top of brownies or cake. Drizzle melted chocolate in a criss cross fashion over frosting. Refrigerate.

Yields enough frosting for one 9" cake or brownies.

Joy's Christmas Sauce

A truly delicious, rich sauce to serve with the Christmas Pudding.

1 cup	butter	250 mL
1 cup	sugar	250 mL
2	eggs	2
2 cups	whipping cream	500 mL

1. In a 4 cup (1 L) mixing bowl, combine butter and sugar. Microwave on HIGH uncovered, 2 to 3 minutes or until mixture comes to the boil. Stir once or twice during cooking.

2. Beat eggs until frothy and gradually beat in hot sugar mixture in a fine stream. Microwave on HIGH uncovered, for one minute. Beat again for 1 or 2 minutes and let cool.

3. Whip cream until stiff and fold into cooled sugar mixture. Chill until ready to use. Serve over Christmas pudding, mincemeat pie or fruit.

Yields about 4 cups.

Butter Pecan Sauce

Rich and elegant!

³/₄ cup	cream	175 mL
¹/₂ cup	brown sugar	125 mL
¹/₃ cup	butter	75 mL
2 tbsp.	corn syrup	30 mL
¹/₄ tsp.	mace	1 mL
pinch	salt	pinch
¹/₂ tsp.	vanilla	2 mL
¹/₂ cup	chopped pecans	125 mL

1. In a glass mixing bowl heat cream on HIGH 1 minute. Add brown sugar, butter, corn syrup, mace and salt. Microwave uncovered on HIGH 3 to 3¹/₂ minutes, whisking every minute.

2. Blend in vanilla and chopped pecans.

Yields approximately 1 cup.

Microtip
This is an excellent sauce served warm over ice cream, cakes, puddings and fruit.

Custard Sauce with Liqueur

Use your favorite liqueur with this sauce. Be inventive and try a different flavor each time!

1 cup	milk	250 mL
2	egg yolks	2
2 tbsp.	sugar	30 mL
1 tsp.	cornstarch	5 mL
pinch	salt	pinch
1 tbsp.	liqueur	15 mL

1. In a 4 cup microwave measure, bring milk just to the boil (scald) 2 to 3 minutes on HIGH.

2. In a separate bowl, beat together egg yolks, sugar, cornstarch and salt. Gradually beat in hot milk.

3. Microwave 4 to 5 minutes on MEDIUM, stirring every minute.

4. Set in a pan of ice water to cool. Stir in liqueur. Serve chilled or at room temperature.

Yields 1 cup of custard.

Helpful Hint
There are three types of custard. A thin sauce (stirred), a thicker sauce used over cakes and fruit or a more solid baked custard.

As custard must not boil, a medium or low power setting should be used. Stirring is essential during the cooking time. If, however, the custard starts to curdle, it may be strained.

Sherry Sauce

If you like sherry, you'll love this sauce. If you don't like sherry, you'll still love this sauce!

½ cup	butter	125 mL
1 cup	sugar	250 mL
2	eggs	2
1 tsp.	lemon rind	5 mL
½ tsp.	nutmeg	2 mL

1. In a 4 cup (1 L) measure, melt butter on HIGH 1 minute. Whisk in sugar, eggs, lemon rind and nutmeg.

2. Microwave uncovered, on MEDIUM HIGH, 3 minutes. Stirring twice.

Yields approximately 1½ cups.

Serving Suggestions
Serve over baked apples, pears, peaches or sponge cake. Fold in one cup whipped cream for extra luxury!

COOKING FOR ONE OR TWO — INDEX

Cake

Carrot Cake	16
Chocolate Layer Cake	15
Yellow Cake	16

Cookies

Giant Chocolate Chip Cookies	12
Soft Ginger Cookies	11

Desserts and Sauces

Apples in Cranberry Sauce	6
Apple Crisp for a Pair	8
Brandy Alexander Mousse	14
Bread Pudding For Two	6
Chocolate Mousse	15
Chocolate Orange Mousse	14
Coffee Cheesecake	13
Creamy Butterscotch Pudding	13
Nutmeg Sauce	18
Orange Glaze	17
Peach Tarts with Raspberry Sauce . .	17
Peach Upside Down Pudding	7
Peppermint Sauce	18
Poached Pears in Red Wine Sauce . .	18
Rice Pudding	5
Silky Vanilla Sauce	7
Tropical Baked Bananas	8

Jams

Ginger Pear Jam	12

Muffins and Bread

Apricot Fig Loaf	3
Colonial Fruit Bread	4
Jam Filled Muffins	2
Quick Raisin Bread	5
Spicy Currant Muffins	1

MAIN INDEX

A

Apples

Apple Cinnamon Bread Pudding . . .	89
Apple Butter	123
Apple Dumplings in Lemon Sauce . .	87
Apple Pan Dowdy	97
Apple Snow	98
Apple Walnut Spice Cake	33
Dutch Apple Cheesecake	80
Southern Apple Cream Pie	77

B

Bananas

Banana Cake	37
Banana Cream Pie	74
Banana Frosting	37
Banana Oatmeal Snackin' Cake	36
Frozen Banana Dessert	113
Frozen Chocolate Banana Parfait . . .	110
Tropical Banana Pudding	93

Bars, Slices and Squares

Arabian Date Slice	66
Butterscotch Brownies	61
Butterscotch Raisin Slice	62
Chewy Bars	55
Chocolate Apricot Bars	58
Chocolate Brownies	61
Chocolate Oatmeal Brownies	60
Coconut Topped Raisin Bars	57
Crunchy Rhubarb Slice	65
Dream Squares	67
Gambier Bars	59
Lemon Blueberry Crunch	65
Nanaimo Bars	56

Breads, Muffins and Coffee Cakes

Bran Muffins	25
Cranberry Orange Bread	19
Carrot Muffins (Cream Cheese Frosting)	22
Frozen Blueberry Johnny Cake	32
Fruit Topped Coffee Cake	29
Graham Wafer Crumb Muffins	23
Hawaiian Coffee Cake	30
Honeyed Gingerbread Muffins	21
Johnny Cake	32
Orange Walnut Coffee Cake	31
Quickie Cinnamon Buns	20
Shirley's Pumpkin Muffins	24
Sugar and Spice Coffee Cake	26

Brownies

Butterscotch Brownies	61
Chocolate Brownies	61
Chocolate Oatmeal Brownies	60

C

Cakes

Apple Walnut Spice Cake	33
Banana Cake	37
Banana Oatmeal Snackin' Cake	36
Beer Fruitcake	54
Carrot Gingercake With Lemon Sauce	40
Chocolate Almond Snackin' Cake . .	53
Cinnamon Bundt Cake	39
Dark Chocolate Layer Cake	47
Date Nut Ring Loaf	51
Diet Cola Cupcakes	49
Granola Carrot Cake	35
Ginger Cake	40

Great Grandma's Sheepwagon
    Carrot Cake 34
Johnny Cake 32
Johnny Cake with Frozen
    Blueberries 32
Lazy Daisy Cake 42
Leanne's Chocolate Chip
    Pumpkin Loaf 50
Lemon Walnut Cake 43
Mary's Butterfly Cupcakes 48
Moist Ginger Date Cake 41
Orange Coconut Cake 44
Orange Gingercake with
    Ginger Cream 40
Peanut Butter Cake 52
Pineapple Cake 36
Pineapple Topped Cake 38
Plain Vanilla Cake 44
Pumpkin Loaf 50

Candies
Almond Butter Crunch 130
Butter Pecan Fudge 129
Butterscotch Candy 133
Caramel Corn 133
Chocolate Peanut Butter Cups 130
Chocolate Penuche Fudge 129
Chocolate Raisin Nut Drops 107
Cinnamon Spiced Nuts 131
Creamy Chocolate Fudge 128
Hawaiian Caramel Corn 132
Peanut Brittle 130
Peanut Butter & Prune Chews 131
Penuche Fudge 129
Vanilla Fudge 128

Cheesecake
Aloha Cheesecake 84
Dutch Apple Cheesecake 80
Dutch Pear Cheesecake 80
Pineapple Sunburst Cheesecake . . . 83

Chocolate
Chocolate Almond Snacking Cake . . 53
Chocolate Apricot Bars 58
Chocolate Chip Oat Cookies 106
Chocolate Chip Pumpkin Loaf 50
Chocolate Fudge 128
Chocolate Peanut Butter Cups 130
Chocolate Raisin Nut Drops 107
Chocolate Sauce 123
Dark Chocolate Layer Cake 47
Frozen Chocolate Cream 110
Frozen Chocolate Banana Parfait . . . 110
Nanaimo Bars 56
Maurgan's Frozen Chocolate
    Peanut Squares 111

Coconut
Aloha Cheesecake 84
Brown Sugar Frosting 42

Coconut Cream Pie 73
Coconut Frosting . . . . ·. . . 30
Coconut Milk 84
Coconut, Toasted 84
Coconut Topped Raisin Bars 57
Dream Squares 67
Fresh Coconut Lime Pie 72
Orange Coconut Cake 44
Tropical Banana Pudding 93

Cookies
Butterscotch Oatmeal Cookies 108
Chocolate Chip Oat Cookies 106
Chocolate Raisin Nut Drops 107
Nut Hermits 105
Oatmeal Fingers 107
Raisin Oat Cookies 108
Spicy Walnut Cookies 108
Thimble Cookies 108
Whole Wheat Date Fingers 109

Crusts (See Pie Shells)

D
Dates
Arabian Date Slice 66
Banana Marrakesh 140
Date Nut Ring Loaf 51
Moist Ginger Date Cake 41
Wholewheat Date Fingers 109

F
Fruit (See Individual Fruits)

Frostings and Icings
Apricot Honey Seafoam Frosting . . . 116
Banana Frosting 37
Brown Sugar Frosting 42
Butter Icing 67
Caramel Icing 118
Chocolate Glaze 53
Cinnamon Glaze 17
Cocoa Buttercream Frosting 60
Coconut Frosting 115
Coffee Seafoam Frosting 117
Cream Cheese Frosting 23
Creamy Orange Icing 117
Creole Frosting 115
Honey Seafoam Frosting 116
Lemon Butter Cream Frosting 147
Lemon Honey Seafoam Frosting . . . 116
Mocha Seafoam Frosting 117
Orange Cream Frosting 41
Orange Glaze 17
Peanut Butter Icing 52
Sour Cream and Lemon Icing 118

Fudge (See Candy)

I
Icings (See Frostings)

J

Jams and Jellies

Amber Jam	125
Apricot Honey Butter	122
Peach Honey Butter	123
Peach Orange Marmalade	126
Plum Jam	124
Summer Jam	125
Super Easy Rhubarb Jam	124

L

Lemon

Lemon Butter Cream Frosting	147
Lemon Ice Cream Pie	114
Lemon Meringue Pie	70
Lemon Sauce	70
Lemon Walnut Cake	43
Lemonade, Orange Syrup	127
Raisin Lemon Upside Down Pudding	86
Rich Lemon Butter	153
Sour Cream and Lemon Icing	118

M

Muffins (See Breads)

O

Oranges

Nancy's Incredibly Easy Orange Mousse	104
Orange Chiffon Pie	71
Orange Coconut Cake	44
Orange Lemonade Syrup	127
Orange Walnut Coffee Cake	31
Peach Orange Marmalade	126
Tangy Orange Meringue Pie	71

P

Peaches

Peach Crisp	103
Peach Orange Marmalade	126
Spanish Peaches and Cream	94

Peanut Butter

Chewy Bars	55
Chocolate Peanut Butter Cups	130
Gambier Bars	59
Peanut Butter Cake	52
Peanut Butter Frosting	52
Peanut Butter and Prune Chews	131

Pears

Ginger Pear Jam	12
Pear Gingerbread Pudding	92
Dutch Pear Cheesecake	80

Pie Crusts

Chocolate Graham Wafer Crumb Crust	85
Coconut Crumb Crust	85
Crunchy Crumb Crust	85
Ginger Snap Crumb Crust	85
Graham Wafer Crumb Crust	23
Never Fail Pastry	68
Vanilla Wafer Crumb Crust	85

Pies and Tarts

Banana Cream Pie	74
Coconut Cream Pie	73
Flapper Pie	78
Fresh Lime Coconut Pie	72
Lemon Meringue Pie	70
Maid of Honor Tarts	79
Orange Chiffon Pie	71
Pecan Struesel Pie	75
Pineapple Sunburst Cheesecake	83
Pumpkin Orange Chiffon Pie	76
Shoofly Pie	96
Strawberry Pie with Cranberry Glaze	69
Southern Apple Cream Pie	77
Tangy Orange Meringue Pie	71

Pineapple

Aloha Cheesecake	84
Amber Jam	125
Pineapple Bread Pudding	90
Pineapple Cake	36
Pineapple Filling	143
Pineapple Sunburst Cheesecake	83
Pineapple Topped Cake	38
Pineapple Whip	112
Summer Jam	125

Puddings and Desserts

Apple Cinnamon Bread Pudding	89
Apple Dumplings in Lemon Sauce	87
Apple Pan Dowdy	97
Apple Snow	98
Blueberry Crisp	102
Chinese Almond Jello	94
Creamy Butterscotch Pudding	13
Frozen Banana Dessert	113
Frozen Chocolate Banana Parfait	110
Frozen Chocolate Cream	110
Fruit Tapioca Pudding	98
Genevieve's Carrot Pudding	91
Lemon Ice Cream Pie	56
Maurgan's Frozen Chocolate Peanut Squares	111
Nancy's Incredibly Easy Orange Mousse	104
Old Fashioned Washington Pudding	88
Peach Crisp	103
Pear Gingerbread Pudding with Lemon Sauce	92
Pineapple Bread Pudding	90
Pineapple Whip	112
Raisin Lemon Upside Down Pudding	86
Rhubarb Puff	101
Rhubarb Torte	95
Shoofly Pie	96
Spanish Peaches and Cream	94

167

Strawberry Whip 112
Tapioca, Fruited 98
Tropical Banana Pudding 93

Pumpkin
Chocolate Chip Pumpkin Loaf 50
Pumpkin Loaf 50
Pumpkin Orange Chiffon Pie 76
Shirley's Pumpkin Muffins 24

R
Rhubarb
Rhubarb Puff 101
Rhubarb Torte 95
Summer Jam 125
Super Easy Rhubarb Jam 124

S
Sauces
Almond Strawberry Sauce 121
Apple Honey Butter 123
Apricot Honey Butter 122
Butterscotch Sauce 123
Chocolate Sauce 123
Cranberry Orange Sauce 119
Fruit Juice Sauce 120
Fresh Fruit Dressing 122
Honeysuckle Sauce 120
Hot Butter Rum Sauce 90
Lemon Sauce 92
Maple Flavored Pancake Syrup 126
Marshmallow Sauce 121
Peach Honey Butter 123
Raspberry Sauce 17
Silky Vanilla 7
Strawberry Sauce 119
Tia Maria Pancake Syrup 127

Strawberries
Almond Strawberry Sauce 121
Summer Jam 125
Strawberry Pie with Cranberry Glaze 69
Strawberry Sauce 119
Strawberry Whip 112

T
Tapioca, Fruited 98

SLIGHTLY GOURMET — INDEX

Cakes
Chocolate Zucchini Cake 145
Petits Fours 151
Praline Tea Cakes 146
Upside Down Black Forest Cake 147
Icelandic Vinetarta 148
Zucchini Fruit Cake 144

Candy
Chocolate Brandy Balls 158
Chocolate Rum Truffles 158
Sugared Orange Peel 159

Jellies
Champagne Jelly 157
Sangria Jelly 157

Pies and Tarts
Apricot Honey Butter Cheesecake . . 156
Double Chocolate Mousse Pie 154
Rich Lemon Butter Tarts 153
Nesselrode Pie 152
Prune Whips 155
Velvet Hammer Pie 150

Puddings and Desserts
Amaretto Trifle 135
Baked Custard 138
Bananas Marrakesh 140
Creme Caramel 138
Creme de Menthe Nanaimo Bars . . . 56
Dessert Crepe Batter 142
Fresh Fruit Ring 137
Kahlua Nanaimo Bars 56
Old Fashioned Vanilla Ice Cream . . . 136
Orange Crepes 143
Pineapple Crepes 143
Poached Pears in Red Wine Sauce . . 18
Prune Whip Parfait 155
Queen of Bread Pudding 139
Sherry Pudding 134
Watermelon Sorbet 141

Sauces
Amaretto Applesauce 161
Brandy Cream Sauce 160
Butter Pecan Sauce 162
Chocolate Fondue 149
Creme de Menthe Frosting 161
Custard Sauce with Liqueur 163
Joy's Christmas Sauce 162
Rich and Creamy Chocolate Sauce . . 160
Sherry Sauce 164

Tips and Hints

If honey has crystallized, warm 30 seconds per cup in the microwave.

Molasses will pour easier from the container if warmed 10 or 20 seconds in the microwave.

Tiny decorative candy liners can be purchased at most kitchen stores. Fill with home made fudge, top with a whole pecan or walnut.

Toast ½ cup coconut with 1 tsp. butter in a 2 cup measure on HIGH 1–1½ minutes, or until coconut just begins to turn a golden brown. Stir every 30 seconds. Watch carefully as coconut browns quickly.

Toast ½ cup slivered almonds with 1 tsp. butter on HIGH for 30 seconds to 1 minute until they just begin to turn golden. Stir often.

As chocolate chips contain some paraffin they do not lose their shape when melted in the microwave. Do not overcook and stir frequently.

To thin melted chocolate add a little BOILING water.

To extract more juice from lemons, limes, oranges or grapefruit, place in the microwave for 15 to 20 seconds before cutting or zesting.

Left over toppings and icings can be refrigerated. Make them spreadable by reheating in the microwave for a few seconds.

Soften 1 cup cream cheese on HIGH 10 to 20 seconds.

Soften ½ cup cold butter 45 seconds on DEFROST.

A whisk incorporates more air into egg whites, making them higher and lighter. They are best whipped at room temperature. Warm them in the microwave 5 to 6 seconds before whipping.

Chopped raisins give more flavor than whole raisins.

Microwave dates 10 to 20 seconds to soften before chopping.

Instead of boiling water for jelly, combine one large package of jelly powder with one cup of tap water and microwave on HIGH 2 to 4 minutes, stir to dissolve. Proceed wtih recipe.

Cornstarch has the same number of calories as flour, but twice the thickening power.

Use powdered sugar (icing sugar) to sweeten whipped cream. Since icing sugar contains some cornstarch it will help keep the whipped cream firm.

Spice Chart

Allspice is available whole or ground. The flavor resembles a blend of cinnamon, cloves and nutmeg. Use carefully as flavor intensifies upon standing.

Cardamom is native to India and is the fruit of a plant of the ginger family. It has an aromatic, pungent, sweet flavor. Use with discretion.

Cinnamon is the most important baking spice, distinctively sweet, mildly pungent and spicy.

Cloves are penetrating, sweet and pungent, almost hot. Use carefully as flavor intensifies upon standing.

Ginger has a hot spicy sweet flavor. Crystalized ginger is the fresh fruit cooked in syrup and is used as a condiment not as a spice.

Mace is a fruit of the Evergreen nutmeg tree. The flavor is similar to nutmeg but more delicate. Mace and nutmeg are the only two spices found naturally on the same plant. Nutmeg has a sweet warm and highly spicy flavor.

Approximate Equivalents or Substitutions in Baking and Cooking

1 tsp. baking powder	¼ tsp. soda and ½ tsp. cream of tartar
1 square chocolate	3 tbsp. cocoa plus 1½ tsp. butter
1 cup thin cream	⁷⁄₈ cup milk plus 3 tbsp. butter
1 cup heavy cream	¾ cup milk plus ⅓ cup butter
1 cup sour or buttermilk	1 cup sweet milk plus 1 tbsp. lemon juice or vinegar
1⅓ cups brown sugar	1 cup granulated sugar
1 lemon	3 to 4 tbsp. juice
grated rind of 1 lemon	1½ tsp. juice
1 orange	6 to 8 tbsp. juice
1 tbsp. cornstarch	2 tbsp. flour (for thickening)
12 crushed graham wafers	1 cup
1 cup milk	½ cup evaporated milk and ½ cup water

Treat Your Friends to

Try It, You'll Like It
Microwaved

Please send me _____copies of Try It, You'll Like It Desserts!
Microwaved at $9.95 per copy.

Enclosed is $_____.

Name: _____

Street: _____

City: _____ Province (State) _____

☐ Please check here if this is a gift. A card will be included.

Postal Code (Zip Code) _____

Please make cheques payable to:

V.W. Publishing Ltd.
P.O. Box 515
Strathmore, Alberta
T0J 3H0

Price is subject to change.

— —

Treat Your Friends to

Try It, You'll Like It
Microwaved

Please send me _____copies of Try It, You'll Like It Desserts!
Microwaved at $9.95 per copy.

Enclosed is $_____.

Name: _____

Street: _____

City: _____ Province (State) _____

☐ Please check here if this is a gift. A card will be included.

Postal Code (Zip Code) _____

Please make cheques payable to:

V.W. Publishing Ltd.
P.O. Box 515
Strathmore, Alberta
T0J 3H0

Price is subject to change.